Wide Was His Parish

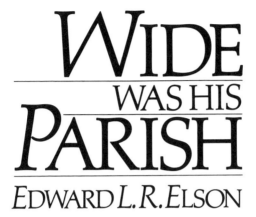

WIDE
WAS HIS
PARISH

EDWARD L. R. ELSON

Tyndale House
Publishers, Inc.
Wheaton, Illinois

Front cover photo by Smith Studio, Pampa, Texas

First printing, July 1986
Library of Congress Catalog Card Number 86-50520
ISBN 0-8423-8205-4
Copyright 1986 by Edward L. R. Elson
Printed in the United States of America

To Helen
lover, colleague, prodder, saint

Eleanor, Beverly, Mary Faith, David
who assured my continued education

Robin, Eric, Melanie
vanguard of the new age

Contents

Wide was his parish, scattered far asunder,
Yet none did he neglect, in rain, or thunder.
Sorrow and sickness won his kindly care;
With staff in hand he traveled everywhere.
This good example to his sheep he brought,
That first he wrought, and afterwards he taught. . . .

To draw his flock to heaven with noble heart,
By good example was his holy art.
No less did he rebuke the obstinate,
Whether they were of high or low estate.
For pomp and worldly show he did not care,
No morbid conscience made his rule severe.
The love of Christ and his apostles twelve
He taught, but first he followed it himself.

Chaucer, *The Canterbury Tales,* **Leonard's Translation**

Prologue

One Lord, one faith, one baptism.

One ministry.

Late one night, March 1969, a young woman struggled in her waning hours against a horrible cancer. I was at her bedside.

Irene had few friends and little money. Years before, she had left her Nova Scotia home for employment in Washington. What she earned beyond her personal needs she sent to supplement the retirement pension of her parents. She had entered the hospital with just a ten dollar bill and no medical insurance. Now she faced death.

At two-thirty that morning my phone rang. A hospital official reported that Irene had died and asked me to help make arrangements with the mortuary. Soon I had the mortician on the phone. Upon learning of the woman's financial circumstances, he agreed to donate a respectable casket and perform all services without charge. I thanked him for his generosity and returned to bed.

At daybreak the phone rang again. The call came from

Walter Reed Hospital. General Dwight David Eisenhower, thirty-fourth president of the United States whom I had baptized and to whom I had ministered, was near death.

I rushed to Walter Reed and there joined several doctors standing by the sickroom. Shortly thereafter the life of the great commander and president quietly came to an end.

We prayed in silence. President Nixon and other officials gathered with us, comforting Mrs. Eisenhower and members of the family. We thanked God for the president's full and good life. Then, silently, we dispersed, some of us thinking ahead to preparations for five days of official mourning and tribute by the whole world.

Later my wife accompanied Irene's sister to the funeral home. They carried with them the clothes in which the young woman's body would be attired for the journey home to Cape Breton Island where Irene would be buried in the country churchyard. As the two of them entered the mortuary, they were met by Secret Service and other security personnel. It so happened that the body of the late president was just then being conveyed into the same building.

Later, the corpse of the young woman left the mortuary in a donated casket. The body of the late president, in compliance with his orders, was placed in an eighty-dollar military coffin and covered with an American flag.

Death is a great leveler.

I think that the events of that morning in some way symbolize my ministry.

The ministry of our Lord and his church is available to everyone, high and low, rich and poor, powerful and powerless.

One Lord, one faith, one baptism.

One ministry.

So it has been. So it will be.

ONE
THE
MONONGAHELA

Pittsburgh was the gateway to the West. Under the huge steel canopy of the Pennsylvania Railroad station, fleets of trains paused to discharge and receive passengers, while giant locomotives were served with coal and water, and fresh crews boarded.

Within the station was a steel gate. Above it was a red and gold sign that read MONONGAHELA DIVISION. Through this gate passengers threaded their way to the trains that operated on the west bank of the Monongahela River. Through other gates passengers pressed toward the great mainline trains such as the Broadway Limited and the Pennsylvania Express, trains that bound the country together on ribbons of steel.

The Monongahela Division of the Pennsylvania Railroad was a controlling force in my early life. Monongahela City was the first Elson family residence. The Monongahela River Valley was the arena of my growing years.

It was in this valley, tamed by the railroads, that Leroy Elson and his young wife, Pearl, settled and began their

family. An engineer for the railroad, my father had realized the dream of boyhood by actually operating an "iron
horse"—feeling the surging power of the huge steam
locomotive with its many wheels speeding over the
mountains and through the valleys, carrying the people
and the commerce of the growing nation. My father was
the local Casey Jones.

Following a snowstorm, I was born on December 23,
1906, the first of nine children. Dr. P. M. Wall trudged
through the heavy snow to attend my birth. Soon thereafter my father's friend, Engineer Harry O'Neil, observed, "He has arrived with pencil and slate, ready for
school." I weighed over twelve pounds, and it was pre-
dicted that I would surely become a heavyweight champi-
on. The house on Chess Street in which I was born was
immediately behind the Presbyterian church—a fore-
shadowing of my future ministry.

Of strong character, my father was a handsome man of
smooth complexion. He was short—5 feet 6½ inches—
weighed a little over two hundred pounds, and wore a
boy's size 5 shoe.

In his daily habits my father was meticulous. He was a
man of orderly mind and disciplined demeanor. He emphasized personal cleanliness and kept his clothes neatly
arranged. He knew where everything was at all times.
When he dressed for a public occasion such as church or
lodge, he was impeccably groomed and presented a
handsome and masculine appearance that I always ad-
mired.

Although a locomotive engineer by vocation, my father

was also an amateur philosopher and a theologian of considerable insight and knowledge. In the highest sense he was a religious man. He prayed daily, read the Bible, and attended church with unvarying regularity. I do not recall him ever going to bed at night or rising from bed in the morning without kneeling for prayer. Outside the home no one would have guessed this, for his religious life was never paraded. He was a man of quiet reserve and natural dignity.

Father was a bit of a musician. He played folk music on a violin and familiar themes on a harmonica. Father showed a lively interest in his children's musical activities. My sister Hazel became quite an accomplished pianist and I began solo work on the cornet and trumpet.

As a disciplinarian he was kind but firm, and only rarely did he resort to corporal punishment. The firm expression, the clear request, and the quiet look were for most of us a paternal command. I received only one whipping—after one of the unforgettable experiences of my life.

I decided to run away from home with my friend Leonard Kosdale. We made our departure on a Sunday before dawn, heading for the banks of the Monongahela River. We "liberated" a boat that belonged to Leonard's brother and started our journey.

Huck Finn could not have planned it better. We intended staying away for some time, just to teach our folks that they were not going to control our lives too precisely—rebelling more against our mothers than our fathers. By late evening, however, we grew hungry and cold.

17

We docked the boat and started home. Halfway up the hill we met my father. He spoke not a word. He simply turned around and walked ahead of us, clearly displaying in his right hip pocket a neatly folded razor strop. With each step of our return journey the razor strop bounced its ominous threat.

Arriving home, I received a lecture about authority, obedience to parents, and living a disciplined life, whereupon the razor strop was applied to my posterior for emphasis. Before Father finished, I reached the conclusion that he had decided to kill the prodigal son and save the fatted calf! Thus ended my only effort to forsake home and parents during my early years.

It is easy to understand why my father was attracted to my mother. Pearl Edie Elson was a beautiful woman. She had a well-defined, classical face framed by auburn hair, a lovely figure and was, like my father, short of stature. An activist, she enjoyed doing things for church and community. Although obliged to cease her formal education before college, she was remarkably well read. She devoured books and magazines and steeped herself in religious literature. A transforming religious experience in Philadelphia altered her whole outlook and directed her activistic nature toward the church.

Mother was the leader of our home because Father was away so much. In the early days railroad engineers left their families, never knowing how soon they would return. As a boy I remember Father going to work and not returning for a week. This was long before the eight-hour workday, the swift train, and the quick return home. Indeed, when the law was passed limiting work to two successive eight-hour days, there was cause for rejoicing in the whole railroad community.

Mother, however, was always there. She was the executive, legislative, and judicial departments of the home. And Father did not intrude when something took place that pertained to rules, regulations, and directions that Mother originated, even though at times he did not agree with what she did. Sunday was regarded as a day different from all other days. Our activities included church services, Sunday school, youth society, walks in the woodland or along the river, and an occasional Sunday evening picnic.

Outside the home Mother taught a Sunday school class for as long as I can remember and was intermittently president of women's societies in the church. She took her family off to summer camp meeting where Father would join us when he could.

Mother had great ambitions for all of her children. She and Father both wanted for us as much education as each child was capable of acquiring. Mother inculcated in all of her children a sense of confidence, pride, and ambition. She believed we could do anything. No allowance was made for failure. Top grades were the norm. Excellence was expected in every endeavor.

And it was Mother who set before us the ideal of service to God, country, and mankind. To spend one's life in the service of others was for Mother the supreme way of life. She demonstrated this day by day in her own life.

She kept a good home and supervised her own children. She also took part in the life of the community and church and was always ready to lend a helping hand in times of crisis and need.

During the influenza epidemic of World War I, Father was the first in our family to become ill, and I was the second. Mother cared for us and simultaneously became an amateur nurse for the whole community. The whole countryside was decimated by sickness and death; many neighbors and friends died during this period. By the time the epidemic ended, she had personally cared for thirty-nine persons. I recall Mother as a great servant of the common good, healing people's distressed bodies without thinking of her own well-being.

When I was four, a new railroad terminal was established ten miles north of Monongahela City, and Father was one of the first engineers asked to relocate. He was prepared to do so, and my parents built their first house in the small new town of Elrama. The frame house with its good cellar and eight rooms still stands—one of the most spacious homes in the community then and now.

Kerosene lamps provided artificial light, and at night adults carried kerosene lanterns. I recall as a small boy having a tiny kerosene lantern that I carried with me after dark when I went out with my parents. I recall, too, Father cleaning the globes of the oil-burning table lamps, and I remember carrying a lamp upstairs on the way to bed. Eventually, as I grew up, the kerosene lamps gave way to gas lamps and, finally, to electricity. Heat was provided first by a coal-burning stove and open fireplaces and later by a coal-burning furnace. Water was first carried in buckets from a hand-pumped well. Later an electric motor pumped water into the house.

Life in a railroad community at the turn of the century had a peculiar fascination. There were always stories of long journeys and new branch lines. New and bigger locomotives were steadily appearing, and with them the strange excitement of wrecks and impending disasters.

My father had the left side of his face laid open when his train collided with another. Once he leaped from his locomotive just before a head-on collision. The dispatchers had sent two trains headed toward each other on the same track.

We learned the language of the railroad. The "call-boy" came to the railroader's home to "call" the members of the crew. The engineer was a "hogshead" because he was ahead with all that power. "Calling the dog" was the engineer's long whistle blast summoning the flagman from his distant position behind the train. To be "cut off" was to be sent on another trip before getting back to home base. The "roundhouse" was the garage for locomotives. The cars were pushed over the "hump" for weighing.

All in all, we had a happy home life. The second child born was Hazel, twenty-three months younger than I. Then came Warren, who died as an infant; Gerald, who later drowned in the Monongahela River; Howard; Pearl;

Dean; Gail; and finally Roy—twenty-five years my junior. Understanding that in the midst of life we are in the presence of death, Hazel and I sat on toy chairs in the upstairs hallway while the funeral service was conducted for our baby brother Warren in the parlor downstairs, the little casket resting on a table. When the service was concluded, we took our places in horse-drawn carriages for the drive to Monongahela Cemetery. The little white casket rode between the two seats in the lead carriage.

My education began in a two-room school in Elrama. My first teacher, Miss Keaney, lived in our home during the school term. She had a narrow waist and kept her hair mounted high on top of her head. She wore high-buttoned shoes, a long skirt, and pince-nez glasses secured by a chain. This school had four grades in each room. Three grades studied while one grade recited. Our playground was a wooded area intersected by a creek, and our youthful ingenuity made the most of it.

In the Monongahela Valley, winter was a great time for growing boys and girls. The rivers, creeks, and ponds would freeze early and remain hard for the winter. An inlet near the Mississippi Glass factory was sheltered from strong winds by high banks. When the inlet froze, the surface became smooth as glass. After school, a huge fire was built. Young and old alike brought skates, laced them up at bankside in the flickering light, then rushed onto the ice, into the shadows of the winter twilight.

My parents' ambition for their children prompted them to send us four miles down river to the developing city of

Clairton, which had a remarkably progressive school system.

I rode a train between Elrama and Clairton in those exciting days, using a monthly pass provided by my father. The railroad station was a mile or so from our house, and the train left at 7:23 A.M. Disembarking at Clairton, we had a long walk to the Shaw Avenue grade school, but we always arrived punctually—if the trains were running on time. In the winter when there were heavy snows, and in the spring when there were floods, sometimes we would miss half a day's school, a cause of great rejoicing and much fun.

Adolescent courtships blossomed on the train but seldom developed into permanent romances. When I was on a date with the daughter of an engineer who lived in Clairton, we failed to watch the clock. Very late that night, I realized I had missed the last train home. My date said not to worry. She would get a pair of pajamas from her father's room and I could stay in the guest room overnight. When she entered his room and picked up the pajamas, her father grunted, "Why can't a couple of railroad kids keep track of the train schedules?"

The first and primary spiritual event of my life occurred on the eve of a new year. I was fourteen, on the verge of putting away childish things (so I thought), and particularly receptive to the whispers of the living God. I remember that Watch Night service in our home, a time of moving reflection upon my past life and consideration of my future life. The living Christ drew near to my boyish heart, and I opened the door and let Jesus enter. I surrendered to him, and all things were made new in the new year.

High school opened a new world for me. I learned to study and manage extracurricular activities as well. In my first term I learned to play the cornet. I had taken piano lessons for several years, but I longed to play a horn. After six lessons I secured a position in the orchestra and band.

My sister Hazel at the piano and I on my horn gave concerts at social events in the Pittsburgh area. One of the great events in our high school days was a recital that Hazel and I gave over the pioneer radio station of America, KDKA of Pittsburgh. We were announced as youthful artists playing from the studio of Etta B. Duff.

Every home, especially homes in Pittsburgh with growing boys, had at least one crystal radio, made by wrapping wires around rolled oats boxes and moving a germanium crystal across the wires. The sound came from earphones. Bedsprings provided the antenna.

The Pittsburgh papers made much of the young "virtuosos" whose act was broadcast to the thousands of homes that had oatmeal box radios. When we reached school the next day, we were cheered by crowds of students.

Everybody in the Monongahela Valley took football seriously. In my junior year, the Clairton team prepared to play the formidable Monongahela High School team, which had an enormous fullback and a fleet halfback. Our coach believed we could win the game if at the beginning we could somehow eliminate the fullback on the other team. Consequently, my coach decided to train me to evoke a fist fight with the opposing fullback. The object was to start the fight and carry it on in a manner clearly visible to the referee so that the fullback would be ejected.

The day of the big game arrived. As I had been coached, I started the fight with the big bruiser, but alas, the referee saw me swing and failed to observe any belligerence on the part of the opposition. So *I* was tossed out of the game, and the fullback remained to win the game for his team by one touchdown.

I shall never forget my football coach, John Lewis, a tall, rangy, blond youth. He had been a good student and a football star at Westminster College in western Pennsylvania. Although he worked us relentlessly on the field, playing football became what it was supposed to be—recreation. The Friday afternoon game was a real relief after four hard, grueling days of preparation.

But Lewis was more than a football coach. He taught two classes in science and was my homeroom teacher. In those days Pennsylvania law required a two- to three-minute prayer at the beginning of each school day. John Lewis would stand before us each morning and read a carefully selected passage from the Bible and offer his own prayer.

If any man in Clairton deserved to sleep late on Sunday mornings, it was Coach Lewis. Instead, he was up early and off to church where he was a ruling elder. More than any minister or layman I met in my growing years, this man's qualities of manhood and character influenced my life for good.

I also remember a farmer named Leroy Beddell, who from his milk route in our town watched me grow up. Having no sons and only one daughter, he always hired two or three boys for the summer to work his farm. I was one of his employees. When school ended I had the desire to get toughened up for the next football season, and nothing provided a better opportunity than working for Leroy Beddell on his farm three miles out of Elrama.

On the farm we arose at four-thirty in the morning and our first duty was to bring in the eighteen or twenty cows, assist at the milking, feed the horses and hogs. By seven o'clock we were ready to do justice to the breakfast of eggs, bacon, oatmeal, and everything else that was put before us. At eight one of the young workers took the milk wagon to town to distribute the milk. The rest of us did other work. If it was strawberry-picking time, we picked strawberries. If peaches were ripe, we picked peaches. If it was time to mow and shock the hay, oats, and wheat, we mowed and shocked the hay, oats, and wheat. On rainy days we cleaned the barn, churned the milk, made butter, and did the laundry. In the late summer we did the heaviest work of all—spreading manure on the fields for the winter wheat.

Discipline at home, school, and church, coupled with the responsibility of a job, developed in me a desire to make the army my career, and I looked forward to entering the United States Military Academy at West Point. Early in my high school days I developed a friendship with my congressman, put in writing my request for an appointment to West Point, and was assured that I would be appointed after graduation. Then, in the summer between my junior and senior years in high school, I had an experience that reoriented my whole outlook on life.

I was alone at the campground in Sebring, Ohio, where my parents had a cottage. I spent an entire day wrestling with the question of what God wanted me to do with my life. At the end of a day of meditating, reflecting, and praying, it became clear to me that I was being led into the Christian ministry. This had always been an alternative to the military life, but now this quiet, personal, spiritual encounter with the living Lord was the crisis moment of my teenage years. Churning thoughts, turbulent feelings, conflicting drives, and competing forces all rose within me.

Before the day had ended, however, there swept over me a sense of purpose—a dominating drive to equip myself for the ministry and to fulfill this high calling to the best of my abilities.

Strangely enough, I never needed to reconsider this

first decision. I did not choose the Christian ministry; Christ chose me. God today still breaks through and summons young men and women into his work. They know that for them there are no alternatives.

Early in the summer of 1924 I applied to Asbury College in Kentucky but had few funds with which to pay my expenses. Fortunately, I had continued my musical studies. I auditioned for the college orchestra and band and received a music scholarship for my freshman year.

Life in college was demanding. In addition to my scholarship and the cash I had saved from summer jobs, wages were earned as a janitor on the first floor of Morrison Hall, my college residence. For this work, which required about an hour and a half a day, I was paid twenty-five cents an hour. I held this job for my first three years of college.

I had made a resolution at the beginning of my freshman year not to become excessively involved in extracurricular activities, and thus had somewhat withdrawn from them during most of my freshman year. However, by the end of that year some schoolmates who had learned of my high school activities elected me sophomore class president. From then on, participation in extracurricular activities became more intense and frequent. In addition to playing in the orchestra and band and serving as president of my class, I was a member of the student council and a member of the debating society, which took very seriously the art of public speech and argumentation. There we devoted ourselves to the art of logical and persuasive public address, and the proper movement of ideas in oral communication. Our varsity team took on and won debates with varsity debaters from assorted universities and colleges. Asbury debating teams were for many years the champions of the state.

That year my sophomore class adopted a goal of "100% for Christ," challenging each person to profess faith in Jesus Christ as Lord and Savior. Although early in the fall term there were some unbelievers, by Christmas every member of the class was a committed Christian. A newspaper columnist contrasted our class with students on other campuses whose chief ambition was to swallow the greatest number of live goldfish.

Asbury College was rich in opportunities for spiritual growth. We had mandatory daily chapel services in which hymns and prayers set the uplifting spiritual tone for the day. The president of the college, a member of the faculty, or a visiting speaker gave a brief sermon, an exposition of a biblical passage, or a missionary address. Some of these addresses and sermons were delivered by speakers of world eminence.

I remember a message delivered by Dr. Henry Clay Morrison, president of Asbury my first year. He was the greatest open-air speaker of that era, a distinguished interpreter of the Scriptures and a preacher of magnificent imagery and spiritual power. In a certain way, he was a consummate actor and had the ability to make his listeners relive the great events of the Bible and personally feel their theological significance.

I'll never forget his sermon on Abraham and Isaac. It was so vivid, we thought we were there . . . trudging up the hill with Abraham and his young son Isaac . . . Abraham preparing the altar . . . Isaac stretching out atop it . . . and finally Abraham's uplifted hand holding the dagger. . . . No one else could preach quite like that.

As great as these chapel speakers were, they made less of an impression on me than did one other. One Monday night in my junior year a new member of our class spoke. She led the class in prayer and then gave one of the most moving expositions of some New Testament passages that I had ever heard. She seemed transported beyond all of us as words of light and life came from her lips. Never before had there been a student message of such spiritual power as was hers that night.

I resolved to know this person. Soon we were having dates on every suitable occasion—eating together in the dining room, hiking in the afternoon, and attending musical events and other festivities on weekends. Before we left the campus for summer vacation, Frances Sandys and I were engaged to be married.

In my senior year I became a student assistant in the Wilmore Presbyterian Church near my college where I was responsible for two Sunday evening services a month. On the other two Sundays I went to an outlying branch of the church and conducted a service for some rural people.

When I graduated from college, I attended the University of Southern California for one year for the exclusive purpose of studying under Dr. Ralph Tyler Flewelling. But I became so intrigued by the other professors that I continued my graduate studies there for four years.

My first postgraduate thesis was on the subject of religious journalism. It was a new field, and relatively little research had previously been done. Being, then, my own authority for the thesis, I had a happy time.

My degrees were conferred by Rufus B. Von Kleinschmid. I shall never forget his statement to me years later, which put the matter of educational awards and degrees in proper perspective. He said, "Edward, all college degrees are honorary. Some are earned in course and others are achieved in the public domain."

To that he then added whimsically, "In some countries you are allowed a natural death. In America when you achieve distinction we kill you by degrees."

In May 1929, Frances and I were married. The wedding was held in her beautiful Los Angeles home on Wellington Road. Our honeymoon was a trip in our new Model A Ford.

I began an assistant pastorate in the First Presbyterian Church of Santa Monica. The large, active congregation, under the leadership of Albert Joseph MacCartney and later by J. Hudson Ballard, indicated the spiritual strength of that church, one of several great pulpits in Southern California at the time.

I had full responsibility for supervising the Sunday school, helping lay officers recruit teachers, developing a curriculum, guiding the young adults, calling on parishioners in hospitals and homes, attending session and board meetings, and preaching several times a month.

Frances also carried a full load of responsibility: teaching Sunday school, leading women's groups, and participating extensively in community affairs. She was a regular contributor to one of the Presbyterian magazines, and these articles became the text of her book *Quiet Hints to Ministers' Wives*, a book touched by her winsome humor and gentle wisdom.

My ordination took place on the Sunday following Easter in 1930. The examining committee took special interest in my graduate work in theology. During a two-day period I completed written examinations, wrote a Greek exegesis, preached a sermon, and submitted a short thesis.

During the oral examination, one member of the committee, Dr. J. Hudson Ballard, posed a tough theoretical question in the field of counseling: "How would you handle a behaviorist whom you wanted to win to the Christian faith?"

The hour was late and my mind was tired. I replied off the top of my head, "Why, that's an easy one, Dr.

Ballard. I'd refer him to you—the expert in the field!" This brought down the house; a motion was made to arrest the public examination, and the vote was unanimous to recommend me for ordination.

TWO
A JEWEL
OF A PARISH

A year or so after our marriage, Frances developed an illness eventually diagnosed as chronic nephritis or Bright's disease. I was in my second year as assistant minister at Santa Monica. I was being approached by three churches—one in Illinois, another in Arizona, and a third in La Jolla—and the bad news about Frances's health was a significant factor in the choice I made. La Jolla was the home of Scripps Metabolic Clinic, which could provide the best possible facilities for Frances's treatment. My years in that jewel of a parish shaped the rest of my life.

I was young when I took that pulpit and was startled, appalled, and terrified by the realization that one-third of the officers in the La Jolla Presbyterian Church were listed in *Who's Who in America*. The congregation was composed of lawyers, physicians, scientists, teachers, business leaders, writers, and artists.

I worked diligently in my years there. I vowed to read two hundred pages a day, and I kept the vow faithfully, enlarging the program with each passing year. As during my last two years in college, I tried to add one or two new words each day to my vocabulary, learning the new words in oral and written communication. So in La Jolla I not only read the pages to which I was committed, but each week I wrote and rewrote the sermon to be presented on Sunday morning.

It was clear to me from the beginning that only the finest efforts of a young minister would be tolerated. It would not be acceptable to give little sermonettes, glorified talks, or exhortations. Consequently, I studied, wrote and rewrote sermons, and unceasingly read theology, history, and politics, as well as fiction. I devoted twenty to twenty-two hours each week to my sermons. This discipline served me well, for in later years high-quality sermons had to be prepared in far less time.

At the beginning of my commitment to the Christian ministry, I aspired to be an effective preacher—not just tolerable or acceptable, but effective. No man has the right to twenty minutes of another person's Sunday unless he has an authentic word from above.

Sermons come out of a man's life. Good preaching depends more on what a man is himself than on academic preparation, accumulated reading, and years of experience. What a man is at the center of his being will largely determine what he becomes in the pulpit.

The channel of music is an instrument or voice. The channel of God's Word is the cleansed, unfettered personality of the preacher. He is in tune with the Infinite, at home with both the visible and the invisible—a man saturated with the mind and spirit and love of Jesus Christ.

Frances's health continued to deteriorate, for there was then no known cure for her illness. People of all ages were drawn to Frances. She seemed to grow more beautiful as her affliction progressed. There was a spiritual radiance about her. People came out of her presence blessed and uplifted. She had a great sense of the reality of Christ's presence. Entering her room, more than once I heard her exclaim, "He's been here! He's been here! Jesus has been here!"

After her death we found in her Bible some verses that described her complete affinity with two worlds—the seen and the unseen, the temporal and the eternal:

Lord Jesus make Thyself to me
A living bright reality,
More present to faith's vision keen
Than any outward object seen,
More dear, more intimately nigh
Than e'en the closest earthly tie.

Frances died in the manse on my twenty-seventh birthday, December 23, 1933.

In grieving over my loss I wrote about Frances, "Our personalities found their perfect consummation in each other. We shared deeply. For two years I carried her up and down the stairs. I do now—in my heart."

Frances's death bequeathed to my future ministry a new and finer texture. Never would I be the same beside a sickbed. At an open grave my words would be more meaningful. The root meaning of the word *sympathy* is "to suffer with." I had walked the path of the sick and the sorrowing, and my ministry derived from Frances's ordeal a lifelong depth and quality.

Following Frances's death, the La Jolla years were for me a time to face the realities of life, a time of growth both spiritually and intellectually. My worldview was expanding; I was becoming sensitive to the increasing turbulence of the world.

La Jolla itself became a balm for my grief. It was indeed "the jewel of the Pacific"—beautiful beyond description, unspoiled in its natural tranquility. My customary walk from the heights of Torrey Pines Road, along the rockbound coast, past the Cove and Alligator Head, by the grassy parkway to South La Jolla, was an anodyne to my soul, certain to drive away low thoughts and lift my vision to the heights.

The La Jolla church grew steadily in size and influence. Its program flourished in all seasons. Forty to fifty percent of the congregation on any Sunday were visitors—in the winter, those from Canada and the East who came to sunny Southern California to keep warm; in the summer, those from inland areas who came to the coast to keep cool. Year after year the same "flock" appeared.

From time to time committees from churches without pastors would visit us and later approach me about my potential candidacy for their pulpits. In 1934 I was approached to be pastor of the Beverly Hills church, which was looking for a successor to Dr. Ernest Howse who had been called to Westminster Church in Winnipeg, Canada. The nominating committee members included, among others, such film notables as Wallace Beery, Norma Shearer, and one of the Will Rogers family.

Since a pastor was needed quickly, I found my decision quite clear. While the church was tempting and challenging, the timing was wrong for me. Frances had died only six months earlier, and I felt a responsibility to remain with the congregation that had been lavish in its support of me during her long illness. In addition, the church had just completed a rehabilitation of the manse. I simply could not go off to another field at that juncture. But few ministers will meet a nominating committee as unique in its composition as that one—nor easily refuse its invitation!

Occasionally Chi Alpha—a small fraternity of ministers—would welcome a guest. Thus Charles Laughton, a famous character actor of his time, was invited to read to us from the King James Bible. So powerful was his flawless and dramatic reading that Laughton was invited for a second program. He then began a regular radio program of Bible reading that continued for a number of years, heard by millions of people. Later in Washington I was to see him sitting in the family gallery of the Senate chamber observing the procedures and studying the eccentricities of some of the senators as he prepared himself for a leading role in the movie version of Alan Drury's novel *Advise and Consent*.

Among my La Jolla parishioners was a physician, Dr. Eugene Perkins, who lived in a home with two maiden ladies, Emily and Alice Page, his former assistants in the

East. Dr. Perkins and the Page sisters regularly attended and supported our church. The doctor also took part in the normal round of community activities. Their home was within two blocks of the manse, and several times a month Miss Emily appeared at our door before breakfast with a loaf of freshly baked bread or a jar of homemade jelly.

Dr. Perkins often strolled along the Coast Walk, stopping occasionally to rest upon a park bench. My father visited us for an extended period while convalescing from a fractured hip and enjoyed sitting on the park bench talking over world affairs with the learned Dr. Perkins.

Unfortunately, Dr. Perkins became very ill and was not given much hope to live.

One morning Dr. J. T. Lipe, a young physician and an officer of the church, phoned me for an appointment about an urgent matter. When he entered my study, he dropped into a comfortable chair and said, "Well, Ed, you and I are about to share in a bizarre experience. Dr. Perkins is not a man, but a woman."

I stared at him in disbelief.

"She has practiced medicine in the guise of a man for a lifetime. Soon you will be conducting her funeral, with everyone believing her to be a man. This will need careful handling."

A few days later Dr. Perkins died and the body was taken to Bonham's Mortuary in San Diego. In Bonham's chapel, among my parishioners and friends, I conducted a formal funeral service for Dr. Perkins, never referring to "him" or "her" but always to "the doctor."

After this Saturday morning service I went to a San Diego State College football game. As I entered the stadium, paperboys were calling out the sensational news of the masquerading doctor. The banner headline read REVELATION! Neither Dr. Lipe nor I had disclosed the story to anyone at any time. Dr. Lipe, of course, had signed the death certificate of a female and, under these circumstances, the coroner made an investigation. It was he who had revealed the story. The sensational news spread rapidly across the country.

What we were able to learn was that Dr. Perkins had graduated from medical school to begin practice in upper New York state at a time when women physicians were not vocationally accepted by the public. The young woman physician disappeared, and a male Dr. Perkins was soon practicing medicine in Cleveland. She went through her professional career and years of retirement without ever revealing that she was a woman.

In the course of time I had accumulated many newspaper clippings about Dr. Perkins. One day I put some of them in an envelope and sent them to my father back in Pennsylvania with the comment, "Now, Dad, we can understand why you so greatly enjoyed your visits with Dr. Perkins on the park bench."

For me the three-year period from 1934 to 1937 was a lonely time of transition. But it was also a time of social opportunities. Without a family, I was freer to attend conferences and conventions, to serve as speaker at summer conferences, and to accompany the young people of

La Jolla on short retreats. I received many invitations to lunch and dinner those days, especially by hostesses balancing the man-woman composition of a party or playing the role of matchmaker.

I was an active tennis player; one of my tennis partners at the time was John Philip Sousa, Jr. And, as in my high school days, football was an important part of my life. Taking a strong interest in the high school football team, I made a point of attending every game, home or away. It soon became known that no one was married or buried by this Presbyterian minister on Fridays during football season.

George Chittick and his wife, Mabel, owned and operated the La Jolla Manor Hotel. When I began my pastorate in 1931 their oldest daughter, Helen, was a stunning sixteen-year-old student at the Bishop's School—an Episcopal prep school for girls, Nevertheless, she remained a Presbyterian and attended my church with her family.

Wherever she was and in whatever she was engaged Helen was outstanding: intelligent, physically fit, beautiful—a tall blonde with a classical profile, long legs, and a svelte figure. She was adept at tennis, horseback riding, dancing, field hockey, and swimming.

When Helen graduated from Bishop's School, she enrolled in a business college for a short time and took summer courses at San Diego State College. At times she attended the Sunday school class taught by my wife, Frances. In 1934, the year after Frances's death, Helen enrolled at UCLA, which was just getting settled on its new Westwood campus. She lived in Mira Hershey Hall, a women's residence, and held a part-time job at the Religious Conference Center.

So it came to pass that on my church business trips to Los Angeles I knocked on the door of Mira Hershey Hall and "signed out" one beautiful coed for a dinner date and, of course, made sure she was returned by midnight. Helen later transferred to the Berkeley Campus. In the three years that followed, as I developed a severe case of "heart sickness," I managed to accelerate my ecclesiastical appointments in the Berkeley area.

The world of 1936 was a melting pot of fledgling political philosophies. Three in particular held the fascination of Americans. Many awaited the outcome of the communist experiment in Russia, curious about the productivity of Stalin's recently enacted five-year plans. Socialism, meanwhile, was taking hold in Europe; it feared the extremes of the communist system and opposed the evils of capitalism, pointing at the Depression in America as a consequence of capitalist greed. Then there was a new nationalist movement in Germany called National Socialism, which proclaimed the superiority of the Aryan race and the concept of the State as a living entity.

I was one of those who were intrigued by these foreign political movements, and probably one of the few clergymen who dared to read extensively about Russia and the economic system of communism.

I was invited to join the American Seminar in Europe

and Russia that summer. It was composed of scholars, writers, lecturers, religious leaders, economists, and business leaders. This traveling seminar offered an exceptional educational opportunity, and it deeply affected my life.

We crossed the Atlantic on the old Queen Mary. I began writing many journals that summer, journals that later emerged in articles and lectures entitled "Feeling the Pulse of Europe," "War Drums Again in Germany," and "Russia—Land with a Question Mark."

The visit to England was profoundly meaningful. Among those we met were members of Parliament Harold Nicholson and Irene Ward, socialists Sidney and Beatrice Webb, and former prime minister Ramsey Mac-Donald.

MacDonald, then in failing health, had suffered much criticism for his socialist leanings and personal abuse by those who had accused him of being a prima donna. He spoke to us briefly about his life and witness and struggles for what he believed would be a better United Kingdom. He said, "I know the reality of evil. I carry the problems with me always. But for forty years I have done what I could. I am now optimistic. We must have faith."

Unforgettable, too, was our visit to Canterbury Cathedral as guests of the famous "Red Dean," the Very Reverend Dr. Hewlitt Johnson. He was dressed in a long frock coat, gaiters, and appropriate apron; his delicate pink complexion and radiant smile were handsomely framed by a fringe of white hair curling over his ears.

The dean was a left-wing socialist. The Church of England would have liked to dislodge him, but once appointed dean he was secure in his position until he chose to resign. In one of his moments with us he said, "The only people I can see seriously interested in the here and now are the socialists who can't be content to leave society as it is and say their prayers in church. We need some hard thinking. Something is radically wrong with money. Ethics must master our money or we will have communism. From an engineering point of view, I'm sure we could have an abundance for all. There is no necessity for private property. We can control money and still have liberty, or we will have communism and sacrifice liberty."

We crossed the English Channel in early July, just before Bastille Day, the French national holiday. The rest of our trip was to be dominated by scenes of political fervor. In Paris there were communist signs and flags everywhere. Half a million people took part in a frenzied parade, carrying signs that challenged LET THE RICH PAY! THE FRIENDS OF THE SOVIET UNION! FASCIST LEADERS AND SPECULATORS TO PRISON! SOCIETY TO END ALL BASTILLES! And COMMITTEE OF THE POPULAR FRONT!

Quite innocently, the day before Bastille Day, I put on a red necktie. When I went out into the street, I found communists saluting me and yelling at me to such an extent I hurried back to my room for a tie of another color.

The French government, struggling to show its power, put on the largest military parade I have ever beheld. It came from the area of the Arc de Triomphe, then east toward the Garden of the Tuileries, in all the color and cadences of flaming nationalism. Marines, soldiers, and navy personnel marched ten abreast. I thought they would never cease. I was amazed at the extent to which the French army was already mechanized: infantry, riflemen, machine gunners on motorcycles, large and small tanks, huge guns drawn by great tractors, and antiaircraft guns. I saw all manner of gadgets for slaughter pass down the boulevard, while overhead the sky was thick with airplanes.

Politically, things were happening in France. The existing government, composed of communists and socialists under Premier Léon Blum, had passed more legislation in the two weeks preceding Bastille Day than former governments had instituted in twenty years. To spare violent revolution, the premier asserted, these reforms—such as a forty-hour work week—were imperative. Ten of us interviewed Blum and were addressed by Edgar Mowrer, European director of the *Chicago Daily News*; Dr. Paul Anderson, head of the Russian YMCA, then taking refuge in Paris; and Jules Sauerwein, a leading French correspondent. We felt the pulse of France and its fragile government in all we heard and saw.

Surprising to me was the strength of communism in the France of 1936. The government, then called the Popular Front, was a coalition of socialists and communists. Signs in villages as we entered proclaimed, THIS IS A COMMUNIST METROPOLIS. On the way back from Château Thierry and Belleau Woods, the great American battlefields of World War I, we passed scores of French veterans returning from Verdun where the "taxicab army" of World War I had stopped the German offensive. Busload after busload of veterans gave us the communist salute of

the clenched fist and sang in chorus the Third Internationale:

It's the final conflict;
Let each man take his place.
The Internationale Party
Shall be the human race.

They shouted, *"Viva le Front Populaire!"*

Entering Switzerland, we visited the Geneva shrines of
the Protestant Reformation, the Cathedral of St. Peter and
the auditorium in which John Calvin proclaimed the
truths that brought reform to the church and fresh vigor
to the Protestant cause in Scotland and Europe. We enjoyed the glorious scenery and found it more difficult to
concentrate on things of the intellect than to respond to
the beauty of the world about us. Nevertheless, I met
Emil Bruner and Adolph Keller who were to assert the
renaissance of biblical authority and the fresh proclamation of Reformation theology.

In Germany we confronted for the first time the realities of the totalitarian state. Hitler had been in power since
1933, and the Nazi Party was still consolidating its position. We witnessed the preparations for the 1936 Olympic
Games in Berlin, done with the strict formalities of the
Germans. Before dawn each morning we heard bands
playing in the streets and saw troops maneuvering and
parading—just as they would later perform on the opening day of the Olympics. Hitler Youth, with flags and
drum and bugle corps, paraded in the streets. Tourists
had to be up early to view these preparations. Early one

morning I heard a knock on my door. There stood my friend Bill Henry, in Germany to cover the Olympics for the *Los Angeles Times.* "How is the view from your room, Ed?" he asked. Together we viewed the troops and spoke of the coming Olympics.

Our seminar group spent some days hearing lectures from members of the German government and from teachers and church leaders. Brigadier General von Mossow, a general in Hitler's SS bodyguard, reflected on the necessity for stability and order in society. Dr. Galinsky, a lecturer at the University of Berlin, intimated that history was being written and taught differently than had been true only a few years before. Bishop Heckel and Reich Bishop Muller had portfolios in the new government, endeavoring to bring the church under the authority of the state. This ultimately led to a great division in the German church when the new Confessional Synod was formed that opposed Hitler and the Nazi regime. Many pastors who joined this group against the Third German Reich suffered imprisonment or execution.

In 1936 we were told it was necessary to understand the immediate background of German life. The Nazis represented a relief from despair. There had been rapid impoverishment after World War I with millions unemployed. There was a wild rush for personal power. Germany had some forty-two parties and its parliamentarian system was a complete failure. Many bright Germans viewed the National Socialist Party as the only way out.

But there had been some successes by 1936. Unemployment nosedived as men and women were put to work in factories, farms, and highways. There was control of prices, property, salary, persons, and work assignments—a control believed to be for the improvement of the new National Socialist State.

The Germans had developed friendly relations with Great Britain and had experienced some international successes. The Rhineland had been reoccupied by German troops who came with imitation artillery pieces and fake weapons, crossed the Rhine River and took possession of the Rhineland from the French. Had the Allies resisted, the whole new movement might well have broken down and Hitler might have ended his days prematurely.

One of our lecturers in Berlin, Dr. Richter, spoke on the Nazi philosophy of history. "There are," he said, "two differing government ideas: the elevation of the individual in a parliamentary democracy, which is chiefly an Anglo-Saxon system; and the German belief that the State is a living thing. The German nation is one cohesive whole of the same race, the same literature, the same language, and the same ideals. There have been three great civilizations in history: (1) the Chinese in the Far East, (2) the Inca in South America, and (3) the European (or Germanic). The Germans are the founders of all modern civilization. We have a duty to preserve this purity and integrity of the Nordic race for the benefit of culture and civilization."

We met the head of the Women's Department of the Nazi Government, Dr. Helen Unger. She began speaking with serenity and intellectual substance. Then she looked down and began to cry, relating to us how her father and brothers had come home from World War I wounded and without work or promise of a future. One of her brothers was killed and all other male members of the family had been wounded. She said that it was an intolerable situation in which she found herself with Jewish men and women occupying the positions of teachers in the university and most other professional positions in the fields of law and medicine.

We heard the Nazi "confession of faith" enunciated by Dr. Robert Lye and other people in Hitler's cabinet. The creed went like this:

I believe in a God who has sent us Adolph Hitler.
I believe that National Socialism is the only saving faith for Germany.
I believe in a God who sent us Adolph Hitler to save us from parasites and do-nothings.
I believe in a God who has sent us Adolph Hitler to bring us beauty and truth.

This was neopaganism as blatant and as blasphemous as anything that the early Christians confronted in the first three centuries of the Christian era. At least nine million Hitler Youth signed and recited this creed and were driven by its spirit into battle a few years later in World War II.

This was the first time we Americans saw this ruthless totalitarian state in action. Jewish business firms were clearly marked with signs on doors and windows, and many of them had already closed. All Jewish men, women, and children were forced to wear the Star of David on their sleeves. We saw stormtroopers carry off Jews, and we felt the terror of those trying to depart from Germany, a nation of which they were once a part.

Our visit with the German people and comments from their leaders would often come to mind in the following years as German life unfolded and war was threatened with each passing month. Our seminar would return to Germany at the end of the summer. But first, a small group of us went to Russia for more than a month, longer than that permitted most visitors in the emerging communist state.

Russia was in 1936 a country with one-sixth of the world's area, three times the size of the rest of Europe, twice the size of the United States, and the largest Caucasian country in the world. It was six thousand miles across and contained 180 nationalities, 140 languages or dialects, and about 100 million people under twenty-five years of age. One who becomes acquainted with Russia must understand that it is not just one national entity, but a consolidation and federation of numerous peoples.

Our journey took us first to Moscow where we remained for eleven days, visiting the historic landmarks—Red Square, the tomb of Lenin, the churches (most of which had been turned into museums), and the libraries and art galleries. From Moscow we journeyed to Leningrad.

It was evident that this beautiful historic city was preparing for war. Troop maneuvers were everywhere. One afternoon while touring the old Winter Palace—The Hermitage—we found the authorities had locked us in with the czar's treasures to keep us from viewing the columns

51

of infantry passing along the banks of the Neva River outside. I stood on a table in the basement, peered out a window, and saw the infantry pass and cross the bridge, partially concealed by smoke.

Most of us, members of the American Seminar, were conservative defenders of American democracy. However, several teachers and at least one politician traveling with us were American communists. I vividly remember sitting with a group of people on a collective farm listening to a Russian expound doctrinaire communism, when one of our party from New York state, who had run for governor on the communist ticket, spoke up to say, "You do not have communism in Russia. If you come to New York state we will show you what communism is."

I returned from this trip more firmly convinced of the strength of the American republican form of government and more vigorous in espousing it than I had been when I left the United States. That time abroad and the many books I read made me forever a student and active participant in world affairs. That experience in my thirtieth year began a lifetime of unusual diversity. Although I would serve only two churches in my fifty-five years of ministry, I would carry with me across the world the gospel message of Christian faith, an informed love for my country, and an illuminated vision of its mission in the world.

With a fresh perspective on my life, I had settled one most important personal decision. I returned to America determined to marry Helen Chittick.

Our wedding and honeymoon were planned for a

week in February when I had scheduled the fewest out-of-town lectures. That week I had "only" three on my calendar. We enjoyed a joyous wedding banquet, complete with serenading Mexican mariachis. After enjoying our honeymoon night at the Norconian Club, we traveled to my first speaking engagement, followed later that week by the other two. At least we were treated as VIPs—at each stop we were given the best suites, bowls of fresh fruit, and dazzling bouquets of flowers. We should have known: Helen's father was president of the California Hotel Association.

I felt my life was complete. Strengthened by Helen's presence, our ministry in La Jolla flourished. We were becoming leaders in an expanding and exciting area of the country. Our friendships grew outside the church as well as within. I was invited to speak at colleges and universities from Mexico to the Canadian border, venturing from time to time to points east. In 1938 I was elected moderator of the Presbytery of Los Angeles, which included some 160 churches and 350 ministers in the region.

Helen traveled with me on most of my trips until the arrival of our first child, Eleanor Frances, and later our second, Beverly Lynn. In La Jolla, a community of many retirees, babies were something of a rarity, and our burgeoning family stirred great interest among parishioners and community members.

Despite the relative affluence of La Jolla, the church and the community were deeply affected by the Depression. We saw the wealthy lose entire fortunes and be forced to live on limited pensions. But in times of crisis, the people of God grow spiritually. In those days, it seemed that the suffering of one evoked compassion from another.

The Depression years required the pastor of a church to be creative economically. The La Jolla church held a significant mortgage at 6 percent interest at the time the Depression hit. At the same time, a number of our parishioners found themselves with investments that suddenly were no longer earning money. The economy was stagnant, dead still.

As mortgage payments became difficult to meet, an idea occurred to me. We decided to sell financial notes to our parishioners at a 3 percent interest rate. In this way they were able to buy into an interest-earning investment and the church was able to pay off its mortgage. Furthermore, many of those notes were never collected by church members but were written off as gifts in wills.

In the final analysis, though, the story of the Depression is not really as much about economics as about people. One person especially made the Great Depression more endurable.

About two blocks away lived Walt Mason, well-known across the country as the author of "Rippling Rhymes"—poems syndicated during all the years of the Depression. He lived in a frame house on Virginia Way, with a study that contained what must have been one of California's largest libraries of Western fiction.

"Uncle Walt" wrote five poems a week. He got his inspiration from daily morning walks, accompanied by his poodle, Pooch. He dressed for his pilgrimage in a clean shirt, tie, neatly pressed suit, and polished shoes.

His little dog was protected from burrs and coarse sand by little handmade moccasins for his tiny paws. Together they followed a regular routine, stopping at the bank, the grocery store, the fish grotto, the mechanic's garage, and the two newspaper offices. By the time they toddled home at noon, Walt had gleaned several good new ideas for his next week's poems.

As an adolescent, Walt had lost most of his hearing when he hit his head on a huge rock while swimming. Medical science could do little for him. He told me once how thankful he was to be "delivered from after-dinner speeches and depressing sermons."

One day he toted two armloads of his best Western novels to the manse with a merry, "You ought to read more of these and fewer of your stale theology books!" He also told Helen she ought not to squander her beauty on a sober-minded young minister when she "belonged in Hollywood." Walt's cheerful poetry and friendship refreshed us as we sought to encourage others through those days of economic difficulty.

I look back on my years at the La Jolla Presbyterian Church with fondness. The people there nurtured me through my time of grief, and they responded enthusiastically to my efforts in ministry. Sermon preparation and reading deepened my thinking, and my travels to Europe expanded my worldview. All in all, those years prepared me well for service in my next parish.

THREE
A PARISH
IN UNIFORM

The Second World War exploded in Europe in 1939.

I had been attending weekly training schools as a reserve chaplain for ten years when the chief of chaplains began calling up reserves for active duty. So when the drafting of young men started in 1940, I informed the chief of chaplains that I would accept active duty. Early in 1941 I was assigned to Camp Callan, California.

Camp Callan was a coast artillery replacement training center with about a dozen chaplains on duty. With the attack on Pearl Harbor and the coming of war, we suddenly lost our troops, shipped out as replacements and fillers for units of the army in Hawaii, Alaska, and islands of the Pacific.

I had been in uniform much of that year and had been requested by my commander, General Francis P. Hardaway, to remain an additional year. I resigned as pastor of the La Jolla Presbyterian Church on the tenth anniversary of my pastorate. Any long separation by a pastor from his congregation is usually detrimental to the good of the church as both pastor and congregation change. The far-reaching consequences of wartime ministry inevitably altered my perspectives and groomed me for my later civilian ministry.

Within thirteen months after Pearl Harbor I had advanced in rank to lieutenant colonel, unheard of in peacetime. The responsibilities of my new position at Fort Douglas, Utah, covered the eleven western states, Alaska, Hawaii, and the islands of the Pacific. I was engaged in the enormous job of organizing our branch of the headquarters staff, which grew rapidly in civilian and military personnel. There were chapels to be built and equipped, chaplains to be recruited. In one year the army engineers built more churches than any other group in the world.

My duties included constant travel to army units within our jurisdiction, dedicating and inspecting the newly built chapels, advising and aiding the many chaplains on duty. One cantonment-type chapel was built for every nine hundred officers and men at a given post, camp, or station. I organized the office according to the functions to be performed. This functional chart became the model for all army chaplains' administrative offices.

After a year at Fort Douglas and an assignment at the chaplains school at Harvard University, I became chaplain of the Seventy-fifth Infantry Division at Fort Leonard Wood, Missouri. This was the first infantry division to be made up of teenage draftees. The average age of all division personnel on activation day was nineteen years and four months.

The division commander was Major General Willard S. Paul, a graduate of Dartmouth and of American University. His paths and mine would be intertwined in the years to come.

I reported to division headquarters and was permitted four or five days to get settled before General Paul requested me to spend a day with him in a reconnaissance of the post. We traveled in his command car for miles, inspecting training areas and equipment, stopping at the kitchens, the mess halls, and various other facilities, and meeting members of the cadre who had already arrived. Late in the afternoon we returned to General Paul's office and sat down to discuss the program for which I was responsible as division chaplain.

General Paul had a long sheet of paper on his desk with a number of items typed on it. As we talked about the religious life of the future division, the duties of chaplains and the role of commanders, I saw him check off item after item until every topic on his agenda had been discussed. When we finished, he said my views and his synchronized well.

It was then that occurred an event that was one of several "coincidences" I would experience throughout the war years.

General Paul received a request from the Presbyterian Commission of Chaplains that I be chosen to escort Methodist Bishop Ada W. Leonard on a recently announced tour of the European Theatre.

Of course, I was tremendously excited about the opportunity. Not only was it an honor to be selected, but I had been in training so long and was eager to see some action.

Procedure, as always, had to be followed, and in this situation it was the responsibility of the division commander to make it official. But General Paul declined to release me. He cited the vital religious program that had begun within the division. He said, "The presence of the division chaplain is essential to the program's ongoing success." Certainly, the division's abundance of teenage draftees played a large part in this decision.

In my place, Chaplain Colonel Frank Miller was sent. He and I had worked together a number of times, and I was greatly impressed. He was one of the finest clergymen in the chaplaincy. Deeply disappointed for my own misfortune, I was nonetheless pleased for my friend's opportunity.

Three weeks later I walked into the mess hall for breakfast. General Paul was seated, reading the newspaper. Seeing me come in, he picked up his newspaper and without a word held up the front page for me to read.

There in banner headlines was the news of the crash of a U.S. Air Force plane. It was the plane carrying Leonard and Colonel Frank Miller. All persons aboard, except the tail gunner, were killed.

Colonel Frank Miller died in my stead.

Later, when the war was over, the remains of Frank Miller were interred in the Chaplain's Plot at Arlington National Cemetery. I participated in the dedication ceremony and said, "Since I was spared, I will preach the gospel for both of us."

Shortly after the division was activated, General Paul ordered a convocation of all officers to report to one of the theaters on a Saturday morning. On this occasion he spoke of his own religious life and of the life that we were to live together as a division. He made it clear that a religious life would be considered a normal life for all personnel, saying, "I commend the regular habit of church attendance. Our ambition is to have everyone in at least one church service each week. This is not simply to achieve a record, but to maintain a life." The commanding general was aware of the leadership responsibility of commissioned officers. "My experience," he continued, "shows that the success or failure of a religious program has a direct relation to the attitude and practice of all leaders. There will be no compulsory church attendance, but I consider attendance at religious service to be part of an officer's leadership, and I make out your efficiency reports!" He further commended the practice of personnel carrying a New Testament or prayer book, and noted that the War Department was providing Scriptures for Catholics, Protestants, and Jews, printed at public expense. He emphasized that he was holding chaplains to very high standards, which he proceeded to implement.

When the general had finished his comments, he introduced me to speak on the role of chaplains in an infantry organization. The response to this convocation was far beyond our expectations. There were officers who said that for them this was the beginning of a new religious experience and fresh dedication, and as the days went on, they grew in spiritual strength and resources of character.

The religious policies that prevailed during the period when General Paul commanded the division were further emphasized when General Fay B. Prickett assumed command of the division. He reemphasized what General Paul had begun, and he published a declaration of these policies that received much attention in the religious and secular press of the day.

After maneuvers in Louisiana, the Seventy-fifth Division returned to Fort Breckenridge, Kentucky, where I received orders to go to Fort Polk, Louisiana, to be the chaplain of the Twenty-first Corps, which eventually trained 250,000 troops. I again went on maneuvers with this newly activated corps under the command of Major General Frank "Shrimp" Milburn.

While in the Twenty-first Corps I developed many significant relationships. General Milburn's chief of staff, General Renaldo Van Brunt, was to become a personal friend for the remainder of our lives. Colonel Percy Thompson, the artillery officer of the corps, and his family attended my chapel services at Fort Polk prior to our going into the European campaigns. One of their daughters, Barbara, later became the wife of John Eisenhower, son of the supreme commander. Other officers of the Twenty-first corps who became our lifelong friends were Colonel Robert Rea, the corps surgeon; Colonel John Arrowsmith, the corps engineer; and Colonel Vance Batchelor, the corps intelligence officer. In retirement all were members of my congregation in Washington at some time or other.

When the call to action came, the corps sailed from New York aboard the Queen Mary, landing at the Firth of Clyde in Scotland on November 9, 1944. We traveled by train to Breamore, England, where the corps had its command post to process all the nondivisional American units in the United Kingdom.

From Breamore we sailed to Rouen, France, on my birthday. I was transported on one of five landing ship tanks (LST), of which only two completed the trip up the Seine on Christmas Day.

According to the command plan for Christmas Eve, the corps chaplain served Holy Communion on the landing ramp below decks to nearly everyone on board. Following this celebration, I was to have been transferred to another LST via launch to celebrate Holy Communion again in the early hours of Christmas Day. Tragically, the other LST hit a floating mine. It sank minutes before I would have reached it.

I do not linger on my day-to-day war experiences. It only takes a few minutes to have enough of that, but when one multiplies combat experiences by 197 days of direct operations against the enemy, they assume a large and memorable part of one's life, out of all proportion to the actual time spent away from one's normal ministry. The campaigns were so strenuous that staff officers, including chaplains, seldom had a moment to think about ordinary comforts or to consider their own welfare and safety. Our job was to be with the troops as pastors in uniform; a staff chaplain had the added responsibility of helping chaplains in subordinate units with their work. The holiday season ended abruptly for our units when we were thrown into position in the Battle of the Bulge as part of the Seventh U.S. Army in the Saarbrucken area.

I shall never forget the shock that came to my jeep driver, Corporal Robert Lignell, when he saw the first young corpses being processed by the burials and graves registration unit of the corps. Bob Lignell already had his A.B. degree from Northwestern University and was an accomplished musician and a superior soldier. As one of my staff, he drove my jeep and trailer thousands of miles in war-torn Europe. He was a soloist, a clerk-typist, and an auto maintenance expert. (Other staff members played the portable organ and serviced the troops with Bibles, prayer books, and tracts.) Once when we were ambushed and drawing fire from German snipers, he handled his carbine with such skill that the snipers were soon silenced and my life, which had been imperiled, was saved.

There were chaplain casualties in the Battle of the Bulge—some killed, some wounded, some with frozen or frost-bitten hands and feet. The Twenty-eighth Division lost two-thirds of its chaplains in the battle, and the commanding general, Cota, was pressing me for replacements that were slow to arrive at the scene of the battle.

For several months following the rapid autumn advance of the Seventh U.S. Army and the First French Army from the invasion beaches of southern France, the enemy had stubbornly held a strong position on the west bank of the Rhine, south of Strasbourg, known as the Colmar Pocket. This enemy salient posed a constant threat to the security of the entire Sixth Army Group.

Operating under the First French Army, the Twenty-first Corps assumed control of a vital sector west and north of Colmar on January 29. Three stalwart infantry divisions—the "Third Rock of the Marne," the Seventy-fifth, and the Twenty-eighth—and three armored divisions—the Twelfth, the Second French, and the Fifth French—unleashed an avalanche of power against the enemy in the bitterest winter weather and over difficult terrain. Within a period of eleven days, the fortress city of Neuf-Brach and metropolitan Colmar were liberated by the hard-hitting American and French troops of the Twenty-first Corps. It was during this time that I was to observe one of the saddest events in American military history.

The Battle of the Bulge had just ended; Von Rundstedt's great surge had been blunted. Lieutenant General Frank "Shrimp" Milburn began an offensive against the Germans in the Colmar Pocket. The general established his command post in the quiet little city of Ste. Marie aux Maines, deep in the Vosges mountains.

The snow had been falling relentlessly for days, and a new and heavier storm began falling on the evening before the Colmar offensive was actually launched. That night General Milburn invited to his temporary quarters—a requisitioned chateau—the generals under his command. Lieutenant Colonel Henry Cabot Lodge, Jr., and Colonel Edward L. R. Elson were the only two guests of lower rank than general. Lodge was one of the officers on the staff of General Jacob Devers. As corps chaplain and because of my personal friendship with several of the other generals, I had also been invited.

When the dinner ended, the officers rose from the table and talked in clusters of twos and threes. General Milburn drew me aside and said, "Chaplain, tomorrow morning the Twenty-eighth Infantry Division is executing a soldier by firing squad for desertion. This is the first such execution since our Civil War. I must give my full attention to the battle that begins tomorrow or I would attend. I wish you would attend as my personal representative and give me a full report when it is over. This is VOCG."

Thus, under vocal orders of my commanding general, I witnessed one of the most historic events in the long years since we have had an army of the United States. It never occurred to me to ask General Milburn to relieve me of that assignment. I was in the military service to do my full duty in time of conflict. Moreover, the men on the firing squad were doing their duty—their painful, agonizing duty. And men—American, French, British, and others—were falling minute after minute, hour after hour in combat.

When the grueling ordeal was over and night had once again fallen, by candlelight and seated at a field desk I wrote what is today, as far as I know, the only unofficial eyewitness account of the execution of Private Slovik. I wrote my own narrative that night for two reasons: first, acting on a sound psychological principle, writing a description of what I had seen brought out an inward burden and much harassment of memory; and second, because it was the first execution by firing squad since the Civil War, it was certain to have lasting meaning in the history of World War II.

The courtyard where the execution had taken place was at the back of the house, next to the mountain. There had been heavy snowstorms for several days, and a deep snow covered the mountains and valley in which the town nestled. Although the snow prevented a clear picture, I gathered the impression that this was a formal garden surrounded by a high gray wall. Areas had been cleared of snow where personnel were to walk and stand during the event.

I did not have long to survey the scenery. Soon we heard the command, "Attention!" The general who saw the officiating party just emerging from the doorway issued the crisp command. Everyone came to attention. An atmosphere of solemn dignity fell on the group. Through the door came the small party of officiating personnel in a column of twos.

The last military police carried the collapse board, which was to support the condemned man if he proved unable to stand before the firing squad. The prisoner's hands had been tied behind his back, and he walked steadily but slowly. The column made a right turn toward the stake. A few steps later the march ended. The prisoner was placed in front of the post, facing us. A hushed solemnity came over everyone.

During the reading of the sentence of court martial, the reviewing actions taken by higher authorities, and the order directing the execution, Slovik looked into the sky. His lips moved in what seemed to be a prayer.

Upon the conclusion of the legal requirements, the MPs completed the physical preparation. Tapes were drawn over the prisoner's shoulders, another about his knees, and another across his feet in order to secure him to the stake. Then a black hood was placed over his head. Chaplain Cummings stepped beside Slovik and began to pray. During the prayer, the firing squad of riflemen and a sergeant from Slovik's own regiment marched from behind the house, halted, did a right face, and took a position directly in front of us, facing the prisoner. Chaplain Cummings slowly withdrew, continuing his prayer as he walked.

The order was issued to carry out the execution, then a quick "Ready. Aim. Fire." There was a crisp crack—an almost simultaneous discharge of the rifles. The black-hooded head dropped to the chest. Three doctors went forward and one by one examined the body with stethoscope and hands.

During this examination, which was the longest part of the ceremony, an MP lieutenant passed behind the members of the firing squad, placing live ammunition in eleven rifles and a blank cartridge in one rifle so that, if necessary, another volley could be fired. During the process of reloading, the lieutenant inadvertently pointed a rifle in the direction of the group of soldier witnesses. I called to him in a restrained voice, "Be careful, Lieutenant, where you point those rifles. One death this morning is enough."

The provost marshal in command of the ceremony announced that the execution was concluded and the personnel could withdraw from the courtyard. The soldier witnesses were marched off under the senior noncommissioned officers. As senior officer witness, I gave the command "Right face; forward march," and we returned to the house where we were immediately disbanded.

Thus I observed the first military execution by firing squad for desertion in eighty years. Slovik, the record shows, had failed his country and deserted his comrades in the face of the enemy—not once, but twice. He had been fairly tried, sentenced, and, before representatives of the very comrades he had deserted, paid with his life for his dereliction.

Still, it was difficult—must always be difficult, I suppose—to watch a man pay so high a price. One must always keep in mind that his desertion may very well have caused other deaths.

If today such a statement seems insensitive, it is mitigated by the memory that the event took place in the bloodiest winter of a bloody war. When it is placed beside the memory of a foxhole hit by mortar shell, or a tank set afire by a terrifying German "88" shell, the execution of

Private Slovik can be remembered as at least a clean death, if not less horrifying.

A most significant episode in my career came toward the end of the war when I made a survey of the imprisoned clergy at the infamous Dachau concentration camp to provide material for officers who later made it part of the war crimes material.

I made the study within a few hours after its capture, when there were still bodies of men, women, and children stacked to the ceiling inside the crematory and as high as the roof on the outside. On my arrival at Dachau a train stood on the spur of the track, beside which lay some fifteen to eighteen hundred bodies. With ox-drawn carts, and under supervision of some of the imprisoned clergy, there began a slow process of picking up the dead and burying them. Disease was everywhere and the possibility of severe epidemics was great. Those of us who went in and out of Dachau in those early hours went through a process of decontamination on arrival and departure.

The clergy at Dachau were treated worse in many ways than other prisoners. In the winter they were required to go out after a snowstorm, overturn kitchen tables, and push the tables through the snow to make paths for others. They delivered soup buckets to the other compounds; if one pail was spilled, it was the men in the clergy compound who received one less for themselves.

The Nazis did extraordinary things to humiliate the clergy. Worst of all were the experiments of a certain Kurt

Von Schilling, a biochemist who specifically requested clergymen to test his theories. He induced in them a condition called cellulitis, a disease of the skin and tissue, and then attempted various kinds of treatment. For studies made on behalf of the Luftwaffe, he placed clergymen in cold tanks simulating high altitude, causing their bodies to freeze. On several occasions Roman Catholic priests were put through this process of bodily freezing and then awakened later to find themselves in bed with women. The alleged purpose of this was to determine the effect of body heat in thawing frozen bodies.

There had been 2,448 clergy imprisoned in that horror camp, of whom 1,008 were still alive on the day American troops liberated the camp. Those men came from twenty-three religious jurisdictions in some eighteen different nations, and I speak only of the Christian clergy confined at Dachau, because rabbis were incarcerated with the Jewish prisoners. Generally these clergymen and members of various Catholic orders and societies had been spied upon by Gestapo in their own churches. They were guilty of evacuating and shielding others from the Gestapo or had given to them some ministry of compassion.

On one of my days gathering the bizarre story of Dachau, I interviewed a man and watched him walk twenty feet away and drop dead.

Two imprisoned clergymen were particularly helpful in my research. One was the Reverend Nicholas Paadt who had been pastor of the great Reformed Church at Zutphen, Holland, which had some fifteen thousand parishioners. He had been in Dachau for three and a half years.

He had earlier been arrested several times by Gestapo "guests" who attended his confirmation classes and scrutinized him with special interest because he was a high-ranking member of the international fraternal order of Masons.

I will never forget Nicholas Paadt in a ragged shirt and a pair of tattered trousers held up by one-half of his old galluses. He carried a bundle of clothes under one arm as he awaited an opportunity to go to the decontamination center before making his way back home. After we had talked, Paadt clenched his fist and banged it on the table, exclaiming, "I swear that I have not done one day's work for the Third Reich in three and a half years!"

"Dr. Paadt," I said, "all of the others with whom I've spoken have told about the necessity of working in order to survive. How does it happen that you are here and you did not work?"

"Well," he said, "when they came in to get a work detail I feigned sickness. They slammed me on the ground. They kicked me in the face, in the stomach, and elsewhere. And after the guards had gone I got up and went about my business. But I swear I have not done one day's work for the Third Reich in three years."

Another very resourceful person was a Jesuit priest named Peter van Gestel. True to the precise methods of the Jesuits, he had a little black book that he kept in his hip pocket. In this book he had noted the arrival date of each one of the clergy prisoners, the denomination he represented, and the day he died or disappeared. When we compared Peter van Gestel's notes with the Gestapo records in the guard's offices, we found them very similar. Peter van Gestel had defied the Nazis by openly and publicly condemning their treatment of human beings. He had condemned the absolutizing and deifying of the German state as being a form of neopaganism that no Christian could live with. The price he paid was long imprisonment.

I spent several days at Dachau, and I was also the first chaplain at the capture of the Lansburg concentration camp. Those and other such atrocities seared my memory. After the passing of four decades, I must repeat what I have said so often. I have never seen, heard, or smelled anything that begins to convey the unspeakable stench and horror of these diabolical dens of evil. When people insist on regurgitating the holocaust and perpetuating antipathies, I am prompted to exclaim, "I was there!"

The battle that led to the German surrender continued. I remember quite vividly that the headquarters of the Twenty-first Corps crossed the Rhine River over the bridge at Worms on Good Friday, March 30, 1945. I could hardly think of anything more fitting as a clergyman than entering this city where Luther posted his Ninety-five Theses that launched the Reformation. The corps swept on through the Bavarian mountains deep into the heart of Germany and then into Austria.

Battered remnants of the Nineteenth German Army fled across the Rhine after suffering an estimated nineteen thousand casualties. The Twenty-first Corps was the first American corps to cross the Danube River when tanks of the Twelfth Armored Division made their spectacular dash to seize a six-hundred-foot bridge intact across the river at Dilingen on April 21. On May 7, the day of the German surrender, as Twenty-first Corps troops penetrated deep into the Austrian and Bavarian Alps, tens of thousands of prisoners surrendered, bringing the total captured by the corps in France, Germany, and Austria to more than 210,000 by VE Day. A large number of top-ranking generals and field marshals, as well as many important political figures, were included in the total. Among these were Field Marshal Von Rundstedt, Air Marshal Hermann Goering, Admiral Horthy of Hungary, Reichministers Amann and Frick. Major units of the German army surrendered at noon on May 6. All resistance in the Twenty-first Corps area ended and orders were issued to all troops to cease fire and halt in place. From June 9 through VE Day to July 2, the Twenty-first Corps was stationed in Leipsig, Germany, and soon controlled approximately eleven thousand square miles of territory in the provinces of Saxony, Thurgungy, and Halle, relieving the Seventh and Eighth Corps of this responsibility.

One of the important questions following World War II was how best to rebuild the German Protestant Church. The church was ruled by a body called the Consistory, composed of so-called "German Christians," some of them members of the Nazi Party and some of them true political zealots. Certainly a strong church was necessary to help piece together the shattered moral values of the nation, but was it wise to allow the Consistory to handle the job?

I was asked to represent the supreme commander General Eisenhower before the Consistory and to deliver to them the decision that had been made regarding the future of that ruling body and the future of Christians in postwar Germany.

General Milburn, my immediate commander, considered this such an important event that all had to be done in a manner appropriate in all aspects. He assigned a junior grade chaplain as my assistant and a noncommissioned officer as a stenographer and provided us with a captured, heavily armored Mercedes-Benz limousine. Ironically, the car had formerly been in the stable of Reichmarshal Hermann Goering. As we drove to the castle on June 15, the car evoked salutes and bows from all of the Germans along the way. We were received with dignity and ushered into a large wood-paneled room with an enormous table surrounded by heavy chairs.

Based upon the elaborate preparations made for us, one would think that the world peace conference was about to be held. The Consistory was convened. I was introduced, and upon delivering Eisenhower's letter I said, "I come to you not as a warrior but as a clergyman, part of the military forces of the United States. I serve men in uniform as pastor. I have been directed to assure you that the supreme commander and all American authorities will allow the German people the same freedom of religious worship that we enjoy in the United States.

You will be permitted to attend divine services and are encouraged to resume, as nearly as possible, the normal worship and work of the German church."

I informed them, however, that the supreme commander regretted he could not approve the convening of a national church convocation for several important reasons. Priority was to be given to the redeployment of hundreds of thousands of displaced persons found in Germany. These people had to be processed and returned to their homes. There were also the obvious requirements of establishing transportation and communication systems, disarming the German nation, and establishing sanitary measures. These and other duties required the prior attention of occupation forces before other things could be normalized. I informed them that in due time the supreme commander himself would encourage a convocation of the German church when these matters had been attended to and when assurance could be given that the convocation would be representative of all the churches in Germany.

It was obvious that the last part of my statement was extremely disappointing to them. This seemed to symbolize the disappearance and the last action of the German Christian Consistory. Thereafter, efforts were made to recognize and reconstitute the German Evangelical Church. It was my privilege in September of the same year to recommend to the supreme commander that authority be granted for a church convocation truly representative of all the Protestant churches in Germany.

After the surrender, I became acting chaplain of the Seventh Army. Under my administration all American chaplains then in Europe were reassigned or redeployed to the United States. In addition, I implemented the rebuilding of the German church.

I had organized with my staff a section to deal with the German church and the German clergy. One of our recommendations was that the Allied military forces should accelerate the processing of those German prisoners of war who in civilian life were clergymen. Many of these were line officers, artillerymen, and air force officers who had for years served as officers of the line rather than as chaplains. We found that an entire German division might have only two chaplains assigned to it, whereas in the United States an ordinary infantry division would have fifteen chaplains, and an armored division as many as ten. We met German prisoners who had not seen a chaplain in more than a year. Many had not received the sacrament of Holy Communion for years. Still others had *never* seen a chaplain.

We were then anxious to have the clergy returned to their churches because no assemblies, conferences, or meetings of Germans were allowed except in churches. We knew that the clergy could have a beneficial effect on the whole nation in restoring morale and direction to a confused populace.

Given temporary duty in the Middle East, I was flown to Jerusalem in a B-25 bomber, where I sat in the front gunner's seat. What a place from which to view the sacred sites so familiar to me from the Bible!

At the time, refugees from Hitler's concentration camps were landing on the beaches of the Holy Land. The British had authorized the landing of just a few thousand, but leaders of these expeditions disregarded orders, and thousands of desperate Jews jumped from overloaded boats to establish new lives in Palestine. Already, ill will had built up between the Jewish refugees and the Palestinian peoples, marking the beginnings of the tension and hostility that continue to this day.

Back home, the Presbyterian Church became increasingly insistent that I return to America. They wanted me to take on civilian status as soon as possible. In addition, they asked me to head up a postwar restoration fund.

The restoration fund interested me because it seemed a natural extension of the work I was doing as chaplain of the Seventh Army. The rebuilding of Europe required massive amounts of money, and it seemed right that the Presbyterian Church would take on such a large and important project. I then became director of the Presbyterian Restoration Fund for the western region of the United States.

I was relieved of active duty in the army, but never ceased being a part of it. I continued with my commission as a reserve officer at the grade of colonel and served intermittently until my retirement from the ready reserve in 1967.

In transition from the military ministry to the civilian

ministry, I recall again the words of the rector of the University of Heidelberg as I listened to him at the opening convocation of the University in postwar Germany. Dr. Karl Bauer was a famous surgeon, and in his first speech he declared:

Theology must be the leader of all faculties. This shall not make us proud, but the more obligated. We have seen in the postwar years in a shocking way what science is without religion. Medicine without God destroys life and helps find cruel practices for concentration camps. Law without God teaches that right is what is of use, pronounces awful judgments, and protects sadism. Philosophy without God falsifies history and teaches militaristic illusions. Natural sciences without God teach erroneous ideas of race and invent the most brutal weapons to destroy life instead of saving it.

America as part of a world in convulsion had to have its part in a reawakening of the true human spirit, as my book *America's Spiritual Recovery* attests. I was ready and eager to be launched into a new ministry for new times. Never before or since have I so clearly felt God's guidance.

FOUR
A CAPITAL
PARISH

In 1946 Washington, D.C., was a city feeling new energy. Its antebellum attitudes and practices were fading. Changes were quickly arousing this once-sleepy capital from its provincial slumber.

Following the war there was a resurgence of spirituality and church attendance. Perhaps the horrors of war had so tried the human spirit that people now depended more upon the Spirit of God. It was a challenging, exciting time to assume a pulpit.

In Washington, the Covenant-First Presbyterian Church was looking for a new pastor. Covenant-First Presbyterian was a church rich in history. It was formed in 1930 by the union of two congregations, the Church of the Covenant and the First Presbyterian Church, each of which traces its genealogy to the early years of the United States.

The First Presbyterian Church was formed in the 1790s by a group of Scottish stonemasons who were involved in the construction of the White House. They first gathered to worship in a carpenter's shed on the White House grounds. The Reverend John Brackenridge served as first pastor and, interestingly, also served as chaplain of the United States Senate for three years.

The Church of the Covenant was formed in 1883 by a group of eleven men who met in the home of Supreme Court Justice William Strong. Four years later, a gray romanesque stone church was erected on Connecticut Avenue—the same building in which the congregation met in 1946. At times, the Church of the Covenant was dubbed "Church of the Government" for all of the government leaders who worshiped there.

In fact, both churches enjoyed the fellowship and worship of a virtual parade of presidents, senators, generals, admirals, and other leaders. Andrew Jackson, James Polk, Franklin Pierce, Grover Cleveland, Benjamin Harrison, Daniel Webster, Henry Clay, John Hay, and Ulysses Grant had attended one church or the other at some time.

I discovered my candidacy for the pastorate of Covenant-First Presbyterian Church quite by accident. We were living in San Francisco at the time, and Helen was expecting our third child. I had been hard at work directing the efforts of the Presbyterian postwar restoration fund. This was a temporary position, I knew, so I was already considering several pulpits and even a few college presidencies.

One night in April we were visited by Dr. Arnaud Marts, then professional consultant for the restoration fund. In the course of our discussion he said, "You know, Ed, you're the leading candidate for the pastorate of Covenant-First Presbyterian in Washington."

I had heard no such news—not even indirectly through the church grapevine. It was true, however, that the former pastor of Covenant-First Presbyterian was Dr. McCartney, under whom I had once served as assistant pastor.

The nominating committee, chaired by Judge Paul Walker, chairman of the Federal Communications Commission, took several months investigating me. On the committee was Temple Bailey, author of twenty-six novels and a contributing editor to *Cosmopolitan*. She later became a close friend.

Ultimately, after guest preaching at Covenant-First Presbyterian as well as at New York Avenue Presbyterian, I received the invitation. Paul Walker called me from Washington and said, "We have unanimously elected you our next pastor. A good spirit prevails."

I was eager for this new challenge, but also terrified to assume such awesome responsibility and a pulpit that was so much in the public view. I realized I was stepping into decades of tradition. My parishioners would be government leaders, even presidents. Of course, I accepted. And I occupied that pulpit for the rest of my life as a Presbyterian pastor and pastor emeritus.

Covenant-First Presbyterian Church was unique in yet another way. The General Assembly of the Presbyterian Church had first considered a national church in the nation's capital as far back as 1803. In 1927 a commission was appointed to bring this concept to fulfillment. Then in 1930, the Covenant-First Presbyterian Church was designated to become the National Presbyterian Church, symbolically to represent all Presbyterian churches in the country.

But financial setbacks hampered the realization of this dream. The Great Depression hit, then World War II postponed it even longer. Though designated as such, Covenant-First Presbyterian had not yet been finally approved and dedicated as the Presbyterian Church's national representative in Washington.

Now, as I assumed the pulpit in 1946, one of my first responsibilities was to supervise the transition of Covenant-First Presbyterian Church from a local parish to a capital parish—to stand tall as the National Presbyterian Church. The main event would be a dedicatory service in which the president of the United States, Harry Truman, would participate.

In my first week in Washington, an admiral who was a member of the church took me to lunch to impart to me his wisdom about the task that lay before me. "The nation's capital is like a great theater. A procession of political entities parade across this stage of American life. The lights are turned on for a while. But soon the lights go out, and the actors withdraw. They all need the gospel. Preach the gospel to them, and you'll get home to the politicians."

Sage advice.

Later that week another admiral said to me, "We've

called you here to be pastor to this congregation—the greatest work on the face of the earth. We know it's hard work to come up with a great sermon every Sunday. But we expect it."

During these days of transition, I wrote a number of feature articles in magazines, one of which was published in *Christianity and Crisis* and dealt with the many things a chaplain could teach the church:

The veteran will be more religious in a rather naive and untutored way [than his civilian counterpart]. He will require a masculine brand of religion if he is to be permanently committed to the church back home. He will want a robust and manly ministry. The minister who is merely chaplain to a glorified Ladies' Aid Society will not attract him. The cloistered theorist, insulated from reality, sitting in his parochial swivel chair, spinning lacy verbiage from his homiletic spindle or engaging in ecclesiastical polemics about trivialities, will not move him. Poetic pastels, however beautiful, may not be sermons to him. He has been brought face to face with grim and awesome realities. He will want to find God in church. He will want to be led in offering his praise and worship to a deity great enough to be God. He will want a church which calls for repentance and provides moral renewal. There is so much which needs to be salvaged he will want a church where salvation can be found. He will want a church where personality is remodeled and character reconstructed. He will want a church where the means for receiving and retaining the grace of God are specialties. He will want a society of believers which assures the nurture of his family in Christian faith and life.

One response to this article was written by Dr. Bernard Iddings Bell and also served as valuable advice:

Thank you for your piece . . . in *Christianity and Crisis*. Keep at it. The church is fast asleep. Blow the trumpet, Gabriel. . . .

Don't underestimate the difficulty of what you're up against, though. You'll have to make your compromises . . . or else you'll remain a prophet and receive a prophet's reward.

There were a lot of us after World War I who said exactly what you say in this article now. Most of them stopped after a bit and played ball with the powers that were. . . . Did they wake the church? Hell no, they did not. Only God can wake the church, and he needs prophets who will prophesy straight through peacetime and wartime. I hope you are that sort.

God bless you brother!

On Sunday, October 19, 1947, President Harry Truman unveiled a bronze plaque at the door of the National Presbyterian Church, marking the church and describing its origin and purpose. He spoke of our nation's postwar responsibility and called for a moral and spiritual resurgence and a more refined patriotism. The president's remarks, given on the front steps and broadcast to the congregation on the inside of the church and to the throng outside, were, I think, among his best public addresses.

Truman, then occupying the White House, was a Baptist and had chosen to worship in the First Baptist Church of Washington. He did so with reasonable frequency until the last two years of his administration when he ceased to attend that church.

Meanwhile, certain events took place in which I had some association with the president. Under the auspices of the National Presbyterian Church, we began an annual service of Intercession and Holy Communion on the day in January when the Congress convenes. The president and members of the Senate, the House, the president's cabinet, the Judiciary, and other leaders in the nation's government were invited to attend this service, planned to be simply what its title suggested: a service of intercessory prayer for the nation, for world peace, and for our leaders. The moderator of the General Assembly came to Washington to officiate on each occasion. Year after year this took place, with a splendid representation of government leaders at a brief morning service which began at 8:00 and closed at 8:45.

The only president never to have attended this service in my pastorate was President Kennedy. Early one November, while I was visiting with him in the White House, he indicated to me that he expected to attend the service the following January on the opening of Congress. "There is nothing in Catholic canon law preventing me from attending a service of communion and intercession. Whether I take communion or not, I can pray."

But he never had the opportunity. Days later, Kennedy was driven in a motorcade past the Texas School Book Depository in Dallas. President Kennedy had from time to time visited St. John's Church, across the street from the White House on Lafayette Square. There he had a prayer early in the days of his administration and signed the guest book. (Every President since Madison has worshiped at some time or other in St. John's Church.)

Mr. Truman not only came to the first of our intercessory services, but he was unfailingly present at all of the others. I usually had the honor of taking our moderator to the White House and presenting him to the president. On these occasions the moderator would bring to the president the felicitations of Presbyterians across the country and assure the president of their prayers and best wishes that he might be given the strength and wisdom to discharge his duties. One of these occasions will linger long in my memory.

The moderator that year was the Reverend Harrison Ray Anderson, pastor of the Fourth Presbyterian Church of Chicago. Dr. Anderson is the only moderator of our church whom I had the honor to nominate for election. We visited with the president at the appointed time in a relaxed and intimate mood. Then, just before our departure, Dr. Anderson said, "Mr. President, when the Democratic Convention was held in Chicago and you were nominated as the vice-presidential candidate, I made the prayers, and I prayed that God would guide you in the years which followed. And I have not ceased to pray for you. In view of the fact that I made these prayers when you received that nomination which ultimately led you to the presidency, I wonder if we couldn't renew this sense of dedication with a prayer before I leave your office?"

Mr. Truman earnestly replied, "I should be very grateful if we could pray," whereupon Dr. Anderson led the three of us in a prayer full of power and rich in meaning.

Mr. Truman was a man of strong convictions. He will be regarded as one of the strongest presidents in our history. He made many important decisions in critical situations—such as in Greece, Turkey, Korea, and the

Berlin airlift—and nearly all of them, in my view, were correct.

In common with many other perceptive statesmen, he had many reservations about the partition of Palestine. For a long time he declined to meet protagonists for a divided Palestine, including Dr. Chaim Weizmann, the great leader of the Zionist movement who was later chosen as the first president of the newly formed state of Israel. Finally, however, upon the advice of his partner in the haberdashery business in Missouri, Truman consented to meet Weizmann.

That day, before Weizmann left the White House, Truman apparently said that if Palestine were partitioned and a Jewish state created in the Holy Land, he would, in his position as president of the United States, recognize its existence.

During the sharp debate that followed in the United Nations, Ambassador Austin had constantly been on his feet asking for a reconsideration of the motion to partition Palestine. When the president recognized the state of Israel, Mr. Austin then stopped speaking to get instructions from his government. The resolution was never reconsidered, and there has been trouble in the Middle East ever since.

Once I prepared an unusual sermon that I called "Christian Quest in the New Year," based on Matthew 6:33, "Seek you first the Kingdom of God and His righteousness, and all these things shall be added to you."

Unlike most weeks, this one found me still attempting to refine the last draft of my manuscript on Saturday evening before supper. I completed it and was ready to do my Saturday night work on the sermon before going to bed.

This sermon was unique among all of my sermons. After a brief statement setting the text in its proper context, the remainder of the sermon was developed around an imaginary stroll taken by President Truman and myself on New Year's Day from the Witherspoon Monument in front of the church down Connecticut Avenue to the White House.

In this sermon I took the liberty of putting words into Mr. Truman's mouth and of conducting with him an imaginary conversation, one that might never have been spoken had we really been together. We talked of his heavy responsibilities, the problems to be solved, the perils to the world. Although I began this imaginary conversation with some diffidence, I became bold and thrust in the words of the Sermon on the Mount—the Master's call to seek first the Kingdom of God. I advised the president to seek God for Himself alone, then to seek righteousness for itself alone, and, having done that, to know full well that God's blessing would be upon us and everything else would fall into proper order.

These were the concluding words of the sermon, and this was to be the chief quest of life for the new year. And thus this sermon, developed entirely around a fictitious walk on New Year's Day, was ready for delivery Sunday morning. Saturday night Helen, as she did frequently, read through the manuscript for correct English, dignity, good taste, and to give me the benefit of her judgment.

Putting it down, she turned to me and said, "You know, dear, I think this is the kind of sermon President Truman would appreciate hearing. Why don't you call him on the phone and invite him to church tomorrow morning?"

I said, "Well, President Truman is a Baptist and, even though he comes to our church on state occasions as president, we just can't call up a Baptist on Saturday night and ask him to our Presbyterian church on Sunday morning."

"Well," Helen replied, "just the same, I'm going to pray about it."

The manuscript was put back on my desk at the manse. A little later we went to sleep and had a fine night's rest. Sunday morning came and I stood in the church with my manuscript, hymnal, and prayer book in hand, and proceeded to the church hall where the choir had assembled to form the procession.

Dr. Thomas Stone, my able assistant, came down the stairs on the opposite side of the church, sidled up beside me and whispered in my ear, "Dr. Elson, President Truman is walking down N Street outside the church. Do you suppose he might be coming to our church service?"

This was ten minutes before the nine o'clock service was to begin. If I had been struck by lightning or by some real cosmic disaster, I could not have been more deeply moved than at that moment, for I remembered that my wife had prayed that he would come to church. I was suddenly reminded of God's work in directing the actions of our nation's leaders. But then I also remembered that the president was in my sermon—in fact, he was the principal character.

Thus I not only prayed for the choir, but I began to pray fervently for one Edward Elson, the pastor, and for his sermon, with perhaps a faint hope that the president would decide to attend services the following week instead.

I continued to fret as the choir proceeded into the church. We were singing the hymn "All Hail the Power of Jesus' Name" when I took my place behind the holy table facing the congregation, about to begin the call to worship. As we sang the words, "Let every kindred, every tribe on this terrestrial ball, to Him all majesty ascribe and crown Him Lord of all," I looked down the center aisle and, on the right side, four or five pews from the rear of the church, sat the president of the United States with half a dozen Secret Service men scattered about him.

After the service was over I approached the president's pew to escort him to the street. He stepped out of the pew and advanced toward me three or four paces, grasped my hand, and said, "Dr. Elson, I want to thank you for this service this morning, and especially for that sermon. That sermon surely hit the nail on the head. I feel God must have sent me here today."

Much relieved, I said, "Thank you very much, Mr. President."

As we walked on down the aisle he turned and said, "Dr. Elson, would you do me a favor?"

"Yes, Mr. President, anything you ask I will gladly do."

Then Truman said, "Would you be good enough to give me the manuscript of that sermon?"

"It would be an honor to give you the manuscript, Mr. President."

"Would you do me another favor? Would you autograph it for me?"

"Mr. President, it's usually the other way around; people want your autograph. But since you asked for it, you will surely have my autograph on this manuscript."

On February 1, 1952, I received a letter from the president that said, in part:

I was talking to Sid Souers the other day and he told me how highly pleased you were with my unheralded stop at your church. That is the way I like to go to church. Whenever a fellow goes to church with a lot of fanfare he ought to stay at home.

I learned two lessons from this experience. First, whenever my wife threatens to pray about anything, I run for cover or live in high expectation. Second, if God gives you something to say, you had better speak it at all costs because that is when the Spirit may really be speaking in and through you.

Not until several years later did the president know what had taken place the night before the sermon. We talked together for almost an hour in his suite at the Mayflower Hotel, reminiscing about other events through the years of his presidency. I then related to him the "story behind the story" of his visit to National Presbyterian Church.

I concluded by saying, "Mr. President, you and I and my wife are the only people who know all about this, but I think it's the kind of human interest story that Americans ought to know about, and I've just been wondering if you'd have any objection to my writing this story some day for publication in some American magazine and later in a book."

The president replied, "America hears all the bad things about Washington and learns all the defects and mistakes of the people who live in Washington—and, you know, we really do pray, and we do go to church when we're in Washington. I think that you certainly ought to tell this story. More anecdotes of this kind ought to be told about Washington and less of the other."

Another time, the Reserve Officers Association of the United States planned a banquet to honor Major General Harry Vaughn, the president's military aide. Hundreds of people attended the banquet, held in the Army-Navy Country Club in Arlington. There were cabinet officers, members of the Senate and House, and a host of military leaders. I attended the event as a member of the Reserve Officers Association and a friend of General Vaughn and of the president. Helen and I were placed at a table with General and Mrs. Renfrow of the White House staff, the congressman-at-large from New Mexico and his wife, and two or three others. Dinner was served.

President Truman was presented early so he could withdraw to get ready for the heavy events of the next day. The president had a carefully prepared manuscript in a black book that several members of the White House staff had helped him write, including General Renfrow.

The president moved through his address, paragraph by paragraph, and as he came to express appreciation for his staff, he discussed the right, the privilege, and the authority of the president to select whomever he wished for his staff. All of a sudden he departed from his written text, reverted to the tone of the artillery officer he had been, and blurted out, "No S.O.B. is going to tell me who can serve on my staff!"

It so happened that Drew Pearson, whose writings were syndicated in hundreds of American newspapers, had vehemently criticized the president for having his cronies associated with him on his staff at the White House, and Mr. Truman's expletive was undoubtedly addressed to this columnist, although he did not mention him by name. As soon as Mr. Truman interjected this phrase, however, pandemonium broke out because most of those present were military people who knew what this kind of language was intended to convey. They applauded and applauded. At length when they had subsided, the president, somewhat flushed in countenance, proceeded with the remainder of his address.

General Renfrow, sitting at our table, stuck his head under the edge of the table and put his hands over his ears. He then looked at us and said, "Oh my! That was not in the text of his address. We'll never, never hear the end of this!"

Mr. Truman finished and departed. All the media people dashed to phone booths or took off hurriedly in cars.

The story was out right then and there and was immediately put on the news releases. Before Mr. Truman's limousine arrived back at the White House, Mrs. Truman had already heard a broadcast of the president's words.

Mr. Truman told me later "when I got to the door of the White House, Mrs. Truman was waiting for me. And did I get hell!"

Mrs. Truman said to him, "Now, you're the president of the United States and presidents of the United States do not talk that way."

Mr. Truman then penitently commented to me, "You know, Mrs. Truman was correct, Dr. Elson. It's all right for Harry Truman, a colonel in the army or a captain of artillery, to use this unrefined language, but it does not fit the office of the president of the United States. As she made me ashamed of myself, I repented then and I've been repenting ever since."

One reason I relate this story is because I offered the prayers at the banquet that night—prayers that opened the whole festivity. And I have rarely offered a prayer which was so immediately attended by the reverse of that for which I prayed.

You never know when you attend banquets to offer prayers what else you'll be asked to do. Once, I was at a luncheon at which Senator Butler, a liberal Democrat, was to speak. Butler was called away at the last minute on urgent Senate business. The luncheon guests saw him hand me his speech and ask me to deliver the speech.

Stepping up to the podium, I began by saying, "You've

seen the senator give me his speech to deliver to you. I'd just like to say that what I read to you does not necessarily represent the views of the person reading. . . ."

From the beginning, I enjoyed good relations with the press. As National Presbyterian Church became more and more the place of attendance for leading government figures, correspondents flocked to church Sunday mornings in hopes of picking up a story. Also, I made it a point to make my sermons timely and newsworthy and to address current issues. Consequently, the press found my sermons to be quite quotable.

I felt that we had a ministry to the press. Many correspondents were not religious people and rarely attended church outside their professional assignments. If, then, they were on assignment at my church, I felt I should take the opportunity to speak to them in my sermons as well as to the congregation at large.

It was also an opportunity to speak *through* them. I soon realized that I had the opportunity on Sunday mornings to be a corrective to the liberal and cynical tendencies of the press. If they quoted me in their papers and journals, it would be something positive and encouraging.

Several members of the press were actually members of National Presbyterian Church. Paul Wooten, of the *New Orleans Times-Picayune*, was a ruling elder. Bill Henry, a correspondent for the *Los Angeles Times*, remained a good friend following the memorable time in Berlin when we watched the Olympic parade from our hotel window. In addition, we developed good friendships with Richard Stroup of the *Christian Science Monitor*; Merriam Smith, chief of White House correspondents; Art Buchwald, whose house was situated behind ours in Wesley Heights; and Dorothy Thompson, at one time the wife of writer Sinclair Lewis and later a chief organizer of the American Friends of the Middle East, in which I participated.

In a public ministry such as mine was, funerals frequently became opportunities for evangelism to the press as well as to the public at large. Many people, of course, who would not normally attend church Sunday morning, attended state funerals. This was an opportunity to speak to people when they were most conscious of their own mortality and their need for God. Many, many times our church would draw into its midst people who had first been touched spiritually at a public funeral.

Once, a music critic got into the letter-writing business with the president of the United States.

Margaret Truman gave a concert in Constitution Hall one night to a large audience of family, friends, and others who were interested in hearing the president's daughter sing. All enjoyed a delightful evening.

One of the music critics present, Paul Hume, had once tried out for a solo position in our distinguished church choir under the direction of Dr. Theodore Schaefer, but Schaefer could not use him in the choir. After Margaret Truman's recital, Hume wrote an evaluation of Margaret that was by no means complimentary.

President Truman read this the morning after the concert. With fatherly love, pride, devotion, and solicitude welling up in him, he took his pen in hand and sent Mr. Hume a handwritten letter of indignation, burning Mr. Hume crisply. Hume, unfortunately it seems to me, released the text of this letter to the press, and it was published in newspapers and newsmagazines all over the world.

When this happened I thought that perhaps I should have released to the press my letter from Mr. Truman, so that it could provide a more balanced perspective of the man. Most of his letters were friendly letters of commendation and good will. And yet Truman's letter to Hume that was so vehement in its condemnation gained all the notoriety and, perhaps more than anything else, brought Mr. Hume to the attention of the music world and to the news of the day.

Since then he has been a highly respected music critic and deserves the recognition he gets from all over the world. President Truman was a great and a good man, as well as a man of strong feeling. History, I think, will be kind to him.

In the late 1940s there was in the nation's capital a whole galaxy of great preachers. Oscar Blackwelder at Reformation Lutheran Church wrote about Philippians and Ephesians for the *Interpreter's Bible.* Warren Hastings at National City Christian Church was the star preacher of his denomination. Leslie Glenn at St. John's Episcopal set high standards for Episcopal preaching. Seth Brooks at the Universalist National Church preached in more colleges and universities in his day than any other American clergyman. Edward Latch was the great pastoral sermonizer at Metropolitan National Memorial Church. Frederick Brown Harris preached at Foundry Methodist with profound theological insights conveyed in superb literary compositions. Robert Norman Gerstenfeld of Washington Hebrew Congregation occupied a prominent place among Jewish clergymen of the day and his weekly radio programs brought fame to Washington religious forces. Archbishop Sheen was at the peak of his career. And Albert Joseph McCartney, frequently referred to as the John Barrymore of the American pulpit, was pastor in what later became my pulpit. On any Sunday you could be sure of a good sermon from those sources.

One of the more inspirational preachers in the nation's capital was Peter Marshall of New York Avenue Presbyterian Church. For too short a period the lives and careers of the Marshalls and Elsons would be intertwined. I had preached in Dr. Marshall's pulpit when under consideration for the vacant National Presbyterian Church pulpit. Dr. Marshall took part in my installation service, offering the Prayer of Installation.

Within a few weeks we were working on the same committees of Presbytery and Synod and attending meetings of Theta Sigma, a local organization composed of two clergymen from each of several denominations. We met at least monthly to sharpen our intellects and enrich our spiritual lives.

In Scotland Peter Marshall had graduated from a technical school which featured a scientific or mechanical curriculum. He grew up in one of those Scottish homes that many writers have called Scotland's fifth university. After coming to America and working at odd jobs, he felt called to the ministry, and with help from interested laymen, he matriculated at Columbia Theological Seminary in Georgia in preparation for his ministry.

Often before making his comment on the evening's Theta Sigma discussion, he would preface his statement by saying, "You know, fellows, I missed the liberal arts college degree and have been getting a 'catch-up' education in this country so I may not have your perspective." Then he would go on to reveal some profound insight or make a sophisticated and learned analysis of the topic. He was able to hold his own in any circle in matters of religion and the church.

He was a member of the Committee on Candidates for the Ministry of which I was chairman. He upheld the high educational standards to which Presbyterians have been accustomed but he did so with utmost sympathy and consideration for the candidate. Some young men (there were only men then in the Presbyterian ministry) struggled with systematic theology or apologetics or Greek or Hebrew. He would compassionately pat them on the back and say, "I sat where you sit and walked where you walk and found it a hard way. Keep at it. We are praying for you." Peter Marshall was very human. He had the most infectious sense of humor and the fiercest temper of any minister I have known.

Peter was also an excellent preacher. He could take a

narrative from the King James Version of the Bible and retell the story with exquisite detail and power. He could take a single text, reveal truths hidden to others, and make these truths come alive in daily life. He was not averse to borrowing the homiletic products of other preachers, reworking, reshaping, and refining them, with little concealment of the original author. But admirers would say the original author's sermon had not really been preached until it was uttered by Peter.

Dr. Marshall did not ride ecclesiastical hobbies, nor was he a faddist. He concentrated upon the great truths about God and man; duty and destiny; sin and salvation; the life, teaching, atoning death, and resurrection of Christ. His life centered in the church. Christianity without the church would have been unthinkable to him.

Peter was a manuscript preacher. He wrote every sermon, took the manuscript with him into the pulpit, and read every word; but herein was part of his genius. He knew how to use a manuscript. His sermons were so organized that his paragraphs, sentences, and phrases could almost be seen as they were heard. He wrote in simple, classical English. His sermons moved logically from premise to conclusion, and he preached for a verdict in the heart and mind of the listener.

The Lord endowed "the man called Peter" with extraordinary powers of elocution that no divinity school or speech class could ever teach. Peter had these gifts before he appeared on the church scene, and they grew richer with the passing of time. He was easy to listen to, not simply because of his interesting sermon composition, but because of his manner of speaking. He had a good voice, and he did not abuse it. He knew how to breathe, to enunciate crisply, and to speak from the diaphragm rather than from the throat. He would speak with rising and falling inflections, change of pace, and now and then staccatto. He knew how to use humor and he knew when compassionate words would bring comfort to a troubled spirit. Once in a light moment I said, "Peter, you could read a recipe for making doughnuts and make the hearers think it was religious!"

We had many things in common—dedication to the proclamation of the Christian evangel in the setting of the historic institutional church, love of Scotland and things Scottish—he by birth and migration and I through my mother and her kin who never allowed us to forget our origins. Finally, next to God and family, we both loved America and were devoted to asserting its ideals and values.

On January 4, 1947, Peter was elected chaplain of the United States Senate—but not without considerable turbulence in the Senate. Precedent prescribed that chaplains were replaced only when the incumbent resigned, retired, or died, the office being a continuing office in a continuing body. Dr. Frederick Brown Harris, the distinguished minister of Foundry Methodist Church, was a highly competent Senate chaplain in excellent health. He had already written his prayer with which he would open the new Congress when, on the late news, it was announced that Dr. Peter Marshall of New York Avenue Presbyterian Church would be the chaplain of the Senate when it convened the next morning, and that the majority leader, Senator Kenneth Wherry, would make the nomination as the first item of business. Hearing the news, Dr. Harris called his friend Dr. Marshall and congratulated him upon the new office he was about to assume.

The die was cast. The nomination was made, and the first partisan floor fight of the new Congress broke out over the replacement of the chaplain. Both men were friends and refrained from personal involvement in the partisan fray. Dr. Harris had scores of friends in the Congress and across the country. Senator Wherry wanted to honor his Washington pastor, not to demean Dr. Harris. So the floor debate took place. Dr. Marshall was elected and received the congratulations of his friends.

Dr. Harris comported himself with dignity and received expressions of appreciation from hosts of people. The two clergymen conducted themselves with consummate Christian grace, but no one could remain impervious to the storm. One day during his second week in office, Peter said, "Ed, I'm thinking of resigning. I don't think I can live happily with this contentious spirit clouding the chaplaincy." Soon, however, divine grace and good sportsmanship prevailed and Peter Marshall served as chaplain of the United States Senate with distinction.

On the day of his election I sent Peter a note of congratulations, to which he replied on January 16, 1947:

My Dear Edward: You were very gracious in writing me with reference to my election as chaplain of the Senate. Since they have not had a Presbyterian since 1879, perhaps we could modestly claim that it was our turn.

With the passing of time and his heart affliction imposing restraints, Peter withdrew more and more from some affairs in order to give his waning energies to his primary responsibilities of the pulpit and the Senate. At the January 1949 meeting of our clergy club I sat next to Peter at supper. In the course of our conversation I asked him how he was managing his heart problem. He turned to me, looked me squarely in the eye, and said, "You know, Ed, there will be only one more heart attack."

Within hours after that conversation, very early in the morning, our phone rang. Dr. Peter Marshall had just died. Immediately Helen and I went to the Marshall home and were there when Catherine returned from the hospital. We offered our sympathy and prayed briefly. The untimely death of the young clergyman touched the whole city.

Funeral preparations involved Mrs. Marshall and her family, the ministers, officers and staff of the New York Avenue Church, officers of the Senate, the Presbytery of Washington City, members of Theta Sigma, St. Andrews Society, and other organizations with which Peter had been associated. The senior assistant minister of the New York Avenue Church, the Reverend Robert Bridges, called on me to prepare the service with him.

The day after the funeral when the Senate convened,

the "greatest deliberative body in the world" elected Dr. Harris to the chaplaincy, thus restoring him to the position he had vacated less than twenty-five months before. Dr. Harris was superb in the ministry of prayer for civil ceremonies. His prayers mingled mysticism and poetry. He served until January 1969 when he retired. Dr. Harris's two terms, before and after Dr. Marshall, make his twenty-four years and two months the longest chaplain's term in history.

Not too many years later, when John Kennedy was killed, services were held in the White House. One evening I was asked to be one of three non-Roman Catholic clergymen to pray in the White House for the young assassinated president. I shall never forget that occasion. I knelt on the prie-dieu by his casket and prayed. When I rose to my feet, there beside me at prayer was a black woman, the wife of a foreign diplomat. On the other side was a young boy who had come to pray and pay his last respects to the president. Sorrow united us, as it brought together people from across the world.

Later, the service in St. Matthew's Cathedral was an extraordinarily moving experience. On one side of me sat Martin Luther King; on the other side sat Dr. Franklin Frye, president of the Lutheran World Federation. Three pews behind us sat former presidents Truman and Eisenhower and their wives. On the opposite side of the church were General Charles de Gaulle and the diminutive Emperor Haile Selassie, who had walked together behind the caisson from the White House.

As the casket was withdrawn from the church and remounted on the caisson, I stood beside Dr. Frye. A very tall man, Dr. Frye turned to me, looked down, and said, "Elson, where do we turn for leaders in our day? Look at us. We're supposed to be the religious leaders."

I never forgot those words, as in the next decades we seemed to be installing in positions of religious leadership men of marked mediocrity. And the words of Dr. Frye have been ringing in my ears with greater urgency since then as I watch what seems to me to be deteriorating leadership in the religious and political life of the nation.

There were great preachers in Washington thirty or forty years ago, but, with a few notable exceptions, their replacements have not arrived as yet. The social activist program of the church, wherein so many people thought they could change the world by resolutions, protests, and demonstrations, tended to diminish the development of articulate spokesmen who might really rally people. The idea that to formulate something in words makes it happen is really no substitute for the great minds who once heralded the gospel.

FIVE
A PARISH
WITH THE PRESIDENT

General Dwight D. Eisenhower indicated in his presidential campaign that, if elected, he would do all in his power to end the war and establish peace in Korea. In fulfillment of his campaign promise to the American people, he hastened to make an on-the-scene examination of that troubled part of the world. While the president-elect was absent from the country for an extended period, many decisions pertaining to the inauguration and the Eisenhowers' future life in Washington were deferred, giving rise to much speculation about various matters, including his choice of a church.

Eisenhower was reared in a devout family affiliated with the River Brethren sect. He was steeped in biblical tradition and brought up with daily Bible reading, prayers, and regular attendance at church and Sunday school. At West Point, Protestant services were led by a chaplain of cadets who also supervised the cadets in their religious life. During this period, Cadet Eisenhower was a volunteer Sunday school teacher and attended weekly chapel services.

When the future general was on staff in the War Department, he and his wife and young son, John, lived a short distance from the Covenant-First Presbyterian Church. John was a member of the Boy Scout troop that met in the basement of the old gray stone church.

In speeches that General Eisenhower made just after the German surrender and during the period of his presidency of Columbia University, there was a pervasive spiritual accent and from time to time an emphatic proclamation of Christian conviction and personal faith. And so columnists speculated about the religious life and possible church relationship of the president-elect.

Eventually, however, it was our daughter, Mary Faith, who learned from her friend, Tricia Nixon, about the president's church attendance plans before anything appeared in television or on the radio. At Horace Mann Elementary School on December 19, 1952, Tricia told Mary Faith that her daddy had said that the new president would attend our church and that they would all be coming with him to church early in the morning on Inauguration Day. Thus the neighborhood children "scooped" the Washington press.

Later that same day news stories were released that the National Presbyterian Church had been chosen by the president-elect and Mrs. Eisenhower as their place of worship in Washington. I was requested to prepare and conduct a private service for Eisenhower, Nixon, members of the cabinet and the White House staff, and their families.

An interesting aside to the record is that President and Mrs. Eisenhower selected, from a diagram and a photograph, the pew in which they were to sit for eight years. They chose the sixth pew on the left side of the center aisle. This location, not in the front but not even halfway back, was a convenient place from which to hear the reading of the Scriptures, the sermon, and the magnificent sound of our choir.

The historical records of the presidents of the United States and their religious affiliations confirm that every president had been associated—formally or informally—with a religious denomination. But as far as anyone could document, Eisenhower was to be the first president to be baptised and confirmed *after* his election.

Abraham Lincoln attended the New York Avenue Presbyterian Church intermittently, and was known to attend occasional prayer services. Certainly he was a warm friend of the pastor during his presidency. There are stories to the effect that President Lincoln discussed with his friend Dr. Wallace Radcliffe the possibility of becoming a full member of the church but was assassinated before he met the church Session and confirmed his faith. Nobody knows for certain whether Lincoln intended to become a member of the church. What we do know is that he was familiar with the King James Version of the Bible, that his own writing and speaking style was that of the Scriptures, that he gave great emphasis to Christian values, and that his personal life witnessed to all people who knew him that he was a follower of our Lord Jesus Christ.

Eisenhower was aware of these facts about Lincoln. How much bearing this had upon the Eisenhowers' decision to establish publically their membership in a church, nobody will really know. But only ten days after his inauguration President Eisenhower confirmed his faith and became a full member of the church.

A preinaugural service was held on Tuesday morning, January 20, 1953. The service lasted just twenty minutes. It began with an organ prelude, followed by a hymn, "Our God, Our Help in Ages Past." One of the prayers said in this service seems now almost prophetic of the spiritual character of Eisenhower's leadership:

. . . Grant unto Thy servant, Dwight David Eisenhower, now and henceforth, health of body, serenity of soul, clarity of insight, soundness of judgment, a lofty moral courage, a sanctified stewardship of office, and a constant and confident faith in Thee. Keep him ever sensitive and obedient to Thy spirit. Make him a channel of Thy Grace and an instrument of Thy Power upon this earth, that righteousness and truth, justice and honor may be promoted and upheld among the men and nations of this world. Let goodness and mercy follow him all the days of his life, that he may dwell in Thy house forever. . . .

The president left the service and returned to the presidential suite in the Statler Hotel. There he took a yellow legal pad and wrote the prayer with which he began his inaugural address an hour or two later. Had Anne Whitman, his personal secretary, not been available to type, Eisenhower might well have read it from his own handwritten copy:

112

Almighty God, as we stand here at this moment, my future associates in the executive branch of the government join me in beseeching that Thou will make full and complete our dedication to the service of the people in this throng and their fellow citizens everywhere.

Give us, we pray, the power to discern clearly right from wrong and allow all our words and actions to be governed thereby and by the laws of this land.

Especially, we pray that our concern shall be for all the people, regardless of station, race, or calling. May cooperation be permitted and be the mutual aim of those who, under the concept of our constitution, hold to differing political beliefs—so that all may work for the good of our beloved country and for Thy glory.

The invitation to all the nation to join him in "my own little prayer" before beginning his inaugural address revealed a dimension in Dwight Eisenhower of which others were not yet aware. It symbolized an emphasis during the entire presidency that followed. The decade of the 1950s was characterized by a marked upsurge in religious faith and spiritual renewal. The president, by his attitude, his words, and his practice, became a model of the spiritual resurgence in the nation. His spiritual emphasis inspired and informed all private and public actions of his remaining years.

The world press commented upon this particular feature of the president's inauguration agenda more frequently and with greater curiosity than any other. The society pages and the gossip columnists, of course, commented upon the substitution of the homburg for the high silk hat, and the short dark coat with morning trousers for the official long morning coat. But what really got home to the peoples of the world, I believe, was the president's emphasis upon the necessity of renewing our national spiritual foundation if we were to be good enough and great enough for the times in which we lived.

The dignity of worship and the order of service at the National Presbyterian Church at that time were perfectly suited to President Eisenhower's personal preferences. In one of our conversations Eisenhower said, "You know, I have a congenital antipathy to excessive liturgy." He also pointed out that he found it exceedingly difficult to receive communion kneeling at an altar rail in front of a congregation. If indeed the Holy Communion was commemorating a supper of the Lord, then he preferred to receive communion in the sitting posture, which he believed to be the more normal and natural way.

He pointed out that many people had urged him to join a church before he received the nomination and campaigned for the presidency. He was emphatic in declining to do so under those circumstances. He told me once that he would no more join a church to secure votes for public office than he would join the CIO or any other organization just to evoke the good will of people. He felt that people should vote for him because they believed in him, trusted him, and had faith in his competence and integrity. He shunned the idea that he should capriciously accommodate people's notions of what his church relationship should be.

Edward L. R. Elson, 1967.

First sermon?
(circa 1909).

Edward Elson at the
time of his ordination,
April 27, 1930.

Chaplain, First Lieutenant, Mounted, 1931.

Holding Thanksgiving Day services, Fort Leonard Wood, Missouri, 1943.

The Elson family in 1950. From left: Mary Faith, Helen, Eleanor, Beverly, David, Edward.

October 1947. President Harry S. Truman and Dr. Elson.

President Dwight David Eisenhower with his pastor, Edward Elson, after church April 10, 1955.

President Eisenhower and Vice President
Nixon with families in front of National
Presbyterian Church, Washington, D.C.

Edward Elson offers prayer at the Second
Inaugural of President Eisenhower, January 20, 1957.

The Eisenhowers with Billy Graham and
Edward Elson at the National Presbyterian
Church.

Edward Elson
with Billy Graham.

The president and his pastor after church.

Her Majesty Queen Elizabeth, Mrs. Eisenhower, and Edward L. R. Elson in 1960 after Sunday services.

Helen and Edward Elson with Ben-Gurion in 1957.

Young King Hussein of Jordan.

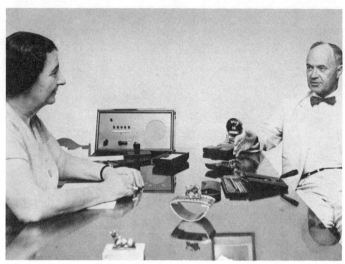

Edward Elson meeting with Golda Meir.

Left to right: William Thompson, moderator of the Presbyterian General Assembly, President Johnson, Vice President Humphrey, Dr. Elson.

Dr. Elson in the pulpit of the National Cathedral conducting the funeral of President Eisenhower, March 31, 1969.

The funeral of J. Edgar Hoover in 1972.

Helen and Edward Elson with Edward Latch, chaplain of the House of Representatives, 1973.

Left to right: Vice President Gerald Ford, Senator Robert Griffin, Dr. Elson, Rev. Robert Lignell, 1974.

Hubert Humphrey with Edward Elson at the dedication of the Hubert Humphrey Building, 1977.

Senate Chaplain Edward Elson with Vice President Mondale.

First Inauguration of President Ronald Wilson Reagan, January 20, 1981, with Dr. Elson at far left.

In Nova Scotia: As chaplain of the St. Andrews Society, dressed in kilts, Cape Breton Island, Nova Scotia.

*On porch of Nova
Scotia home in
August 1984.*

*The new National
Presbyterian Church.*

Helen C. Elson.

Edward L. R. Elson.

Eisenhower was not a formal member of a Christian church at the time he took the oath of office. The president's brother, Dr. Milton Eisenhower, confirmed that the president had not been baptized and admitted to the River Brethren Church in his hometown of Abilene.

Christian baptism is a public occasion, usually performed in the presence of a congregation. In the Presbyterian Church, individuals are baptized during the church service and they are announced as new members before they receive their first communion. The names of all new members are entered in special ledgers and printed in the Sunday bulletin and parish paper.

The president asked me to give him a memo on the procedure. This I did, carefully indicating what he would be asked and what he was expected to reply. He would be joining the church in precisely the same way as any other unbaptized person. Eisenhower was determined, he said, to do whatever must be done to be completely a member of the Christian church.

President and Mrs. Eisenhower met with the Session of National Presbyterian Church in the N Street chapel at 8:30 A.M. on February 1, 1953. Most of the thirty elders of the Session were present. I read these words from the *Book of Common Worship:*

Baptism is of divine ordinance; Christ Himself was baptized and sent out His disciples to baptize men as the mark of their Christian faith and discipleship.

Then I put forth the question, "Do you, Dwight David Eisenhower, confess your need of the forgiveness of sins,

115

and do you confess your faith in Jesus Christ as the Lord and Savior of your life? In this faith do you desire to be baptized, and in dependence upon His Grace, do you promise to live the Christian life?"

The president answered clearly and reverently, "I do." Then he knelt on the prie-dieu.

I offered the prayer, setting apart the water from a common to a sacred use. Dipping my right hand into the water, I placed it on the president's head and said, "Dwight David, I baptize thee in the name of the Father and of the Son and of the Holy Spirit, and may the Lord defend you with His Grace."

Then I offered the following prayer:

Almighty and Eternal God, strengthen this Thy servant we beseech Thee, with the Holy Spirit, the Comforter, and daily increase in him Thy manifold gifts of Grace, the spirit of wisdom and understanding, the spirit of counsel and might, the spirit of knowledge and of the fear of the Lord, and keep him in Thy mercy unto life eternal, through Jesus Christ our Lord. Amen.

One of the elders moved that the president be received upon confession of his faith and baptism and that his name be enrolled. Another moved that Mrs. Eisenhower be made a member upon reaffirmation of her faith. After some words of exhortation, calling them to fidelity to the services and sacraments of the church and to witnessing to the Christian life in their daily vocation, the president and Mrs. Eisenhower signed the membership book and the baptismal records.

The elders gave the Eisenhowers the right hand of Christian fellowship. They then left us to enter the sanctuary and take their places in the sixth pew on the left side of the center aisle.

As was customary, before the celebration of Holy Communion the names of the new communicant members were announced. On this occasion the Eisenhowers were named among those who had been received into church membership by the Session and would be receiving their first communion. This was the only reference to them by name and was precisely the same procedure as was used for every other new member.

The only concession to the extraordinary circumstances of a president being baptized was that the baptismal sacrament was performed in the chapel before the Session representing the congregation, rather than before the entire congregation. This accommodation relieved the Secret Service considerably.

Neither I nor any church official released a news story. But wherever the president of the United States goes, the press goes also. It was no surprise, therefore, that in the back of the church at the nine o'clock service sat representatives of the Associated Press, UPI, International News Service, the *New York Times*, the *Washington Post*, the *Washington Star*, and the religious press. They heard what everybody heard—including the names of new members— and before the late service, the story was being broadcast all over the world. Nothing like this had happened before in American history. Later, a historian on the faculty of the Catholic University in America telephoned me to say that the baptism of the president must be the first baptism of a chief of state since Clovis I, king of the Franks in the sixth century.

So much publicity was given to the president, his marked attention to the life of the church, and his religious values, that handling my mail and the news media became a burden. Hundreds of letters came each day, especially after sermon quotations appeared in the press. My days were quite stressful, particularly when people attempted to use my pastoral office as the means for gaining an appointment with or a particular favor from the president.

In my early conversations with President Eisenhower in New York City, and in discussing his church membership, I had made two promises to him. First, I promised that I would be a faithful pastor, ministering to his spiritual needs and making myself available to him. Second, I emphatically promised him that I would never use, nor permit anybody else to use, the pastoral relationship for any purpose other than religious ministry.

As time went on I came to appreciate more and more these two promises to the president. Not a day passed without good friends, and even total strangers, attempting to approach the president through me. Some wanted appointments to commissions, ambassadorships, or to the White House staff; some wanted to become speech writers; some simply wanted to get "close to the president." Day after day I was able to quote to these supplicants my promises to the president.

No publicity was ever given by the White House or the National Presbyterian Church about the president's attendance at church events. Tradition and etiquette prescribe that the president is to be granted the same courtesy as other worshipers. Indeed, the president was perhaps more comfortable in his Washington church than anywhere else but his home.

The only formal recognition of the president's attendance was a small footnote at the bottom of the bulletin: "At the service in which the president of the United States is a worshiper, the congregation will stand following the benediction, choral amen, and chimes until the president has left the church." Accordingly, I would go down the center aisle to the president's pew and escort the president and First Lady to their limousine.

On Saturday, usually in the morning, I would receive a phone call from the White House chief of Secret Service advising me that the president and other members of the family would attend church at nine or eleven o'clock the next morning. I would inform the head usher and the sexton, both of whom had some preparations to make.

On Sundays the Secret Service would arrive at the church an hour or more ahead of the presidential party. They would "flush out" (inspect) the building. Many times Secret Service agents would be in the building Saturday night. On these occasions when I unlocked the door to enter my study I would be greeted inside by one or more Secret Service agents. Sunday morning a detachment of firemen and uniformed police would be posted at each entrance and in the cellar.

All doors of the church were open to receive members of the congregation until the chief of Secret Service received a radio alert that the president was leaving the White House. Then worshipers would be diverted from the main door to the south entrance. The presidential limousine accompanied by several Secret Service automobiles would arrive at the main Connecticut Avenue entrance, where the presidential party would disembark and proceed to their place in the church. Mr. Bain always sat immediately behind the president, and another agent sat on the opposite end of the president's pew. On Sundays when there were only two or three from the White House, President and Mrs. Eisenhower asked Helen and our family to fill out the remaining places in the sixth pew.

On one of Sir Winston Churchill's postwar visits to the White House, supper on Saturday was ended and Eisenhower and guests were ready to withdraw for the night when the president turned to Sir Winston and said, "Mrs. Eisenhower and I will attend the National Presbyterian Church at eleven o'clock tomorrow. We would be honored indeed if you would accompany us."

Sir Winston grew grave and pensive and then looked at the president through impish eyes and said, "Mr. President, I'm getting to be an old man. Soon I am going to have an encounter with my Maker. I think I had better remain at home tomorrow to rest up for the occasion." Sir Winston remained in bed late, as all his associates knew to be his custom. The president smiled when he related the episode to me some days later.

The president was a good listener. Occasionally he would linger at the door before departing to discuss some aspect of the message I had just given, to ask a clarifying question, or to shed some biblical light upon it which arose out of his own knowledge. He knew the Bible very well, having learned its contents from morning and evening reading with his parents and brothers. If you were to quote a passage, you'd better quote it accurately, for he would know the difference.

In January 1954 I preached a sermon called "The Mastery of Moods" on the text from 2 Corinthians 5:14, "The love of Christ controls us." The sermon had to do with temper and temperament, with criticism and undisciplined emotion, and with how the love of Christ brings an antidote and healing. Self-mastery is not enough; only Christ's mastery is sufficient.

At the church door that Sunday the president asked how soon he could get fifty printed copies of that sermon, for he said a lot of his friends and colleagues could benefit from reading it. The president sent the sermon with a cover letter to about fifty people, and for several weeks I met cabinet members, leaders of the Congress, and military officers who thanked me for "The Mastery of Moods." Eisenhower also circulated other sermons, such as "First Step to Knowledge" on the text, "Be still and know that I am God" (Psalm 46:10).

The president and First Lady had many favorite hymns. One week they took my hymnal home with them and on the index marked some of their favorites—twenty-four of them.

On a Sunday morning when the United States was in
one of its crises with Khrushchev, I looked down from the
pulpit during the hymn before the sermon, and there was
the president lustily and confidently singing "What a
Friend We Have in Jesus."

Have we trials and temptations?
Is there trouble anywhere?
We should never be discouraged;
Take it to the Lord in prayer.

The profundity of this simple, prayerful hymn seemed to
overwhelm me that morning.

Nobody ever spoke to the president about his financial
support of his church. But he read the bulletins and listened to the lay leaders give their annual stewardship
talks. Early each year Brigadier General Shultz, the president's military aide, would deliver a sealed hand-
addressed envelope to me with the request that the contents not be disclosed to any other person but be recorded
anonymously by the church treasurer. In the envelope
was a substantial check or pledge card. In addition to this,
the chief usher at the White House each Sunday would
hand the president a crisp bill to deposit in the offering
plate.

When the annual church fair came, Mrs. Eisenhower
would be honorary chairperson. She always contributed
some items, personally cut the ribbon opening the fair,
and departed only after three or four shopping bags were
filled with her purchases. On these occasions she would
be joined by wives of other persons in the administration:

Mrs. Warren Burger and Mrs. Perry Morton, whose husbands were assistant attorney generals; Mrs. John Foster Dulles; Mrs. Arthur Somerfield; Mrs. Douglas MacKay, wife of the secretary of the interior; Mrs. Wilber Brucker, wife of the counsel for the Department of Defense; and Mrs. Robert Stevens, wife of the secretary of the army.

In the early months of the Eisenhower administration, the country was polluted by the obnoxious antics of Senator Joseph McCarthy. As the hearings went on and the Schine-Cohn claims occupied center ring, I commiserated almost daily with Secretary of the Army Stevens until the day he was delivered from the malicious tactics of McCarthy.

The president refused to get into the gutter with anybody like McCarthy. When I suggested to the president's counselors that they ought to extinguish the McCarthy fire, I was told that liquor was already doing the job, which it finished in a short time.

One of our parishioners was J. Edgar Hoover. He was a devout man and a strong supporter of the National Presbyterian Church. Hoover grew up a member of the old First Presbyterian Church on Capitol Hill, one of the two congregations that joined together to form the current membership of the National Presbyterian Church. He taught Sunday school and later was the superintendent of the junior department.

One of the pastors of the church, Dr. McLeod, had such an influence on Hoover that at one point the young man was considering the ministry. Later, in my pastorate, Hoover served as a leader in the Boys' Clubs of America and also as a trustee of the National Presbyterian Church.

As director of the FBI, Hoover encouraged a healthy home life and devotion to church life among his agents. For many years, I helped lead a special service in our church for FBI personnel and their families.

One year, Hoover presented me with a thank-you gift for my help in conducting these services. He had always joked with me about the file he had on me at the FBI, but I never took him seriously. So it was with a bit of surprise and a good laugh that I opened his gift to me—a pair of cuff links with my fingerprints engraved on them.

Hoover and the FBI once assisted in a ticklish church matter. A young couple named Motherwell joined our church and became involved in a church organization called the Sunday Evening Club, which consisted of young people twenty to thirty-five years of age. The Sunday Evening Club, besides their usual meetings, organized many service opportunities for the young people.

Larry Motherwell claimed to be a member of the CIA, and he told fantastic stories about his work for intelligence. He described being dropped behind enemy lines during the Korean War to collect information about the enemy. Once he came to church with his head bandaged, and he reported that he had been injured in the line of duty.

The church was in the process of electing officers, and the Sunday Evening Club expressed the desire that one of their crowd be nominated for a position of elder. They recommended Larry Motherwell, so he was nominated and later elected.

Motherwell organized a trip to Scotland and was starting to collect money from various parishioners for the trip. Something about this did not seem right, so another parishioner and I did some background research and discovered that Motherwell was a fraud. I called parishioners Sidney Souers of the CIA and J. Edgar Hoover to conduct an investigation of the man. For months, FBI agents attended church dinners and services, sitting near Motherwell, without anyone in the church knowing what was going on.

Some time later, Hoover stopped in my office, pulled out a folder stuffed with papers, and asked, "How did this bird get into this church, let alone get elected an elder?"

The man's real name was John Cavender, a carpenter. He'd never been to Korea. He'd once been arrested and served time for impersonating a naval officer. I called Cavender into my office. I told him we knew who he was and said, "I ordained as elder of this church a fictitious man named Motherwell. I did not ordain a Cavender. The ordination is rendered null and void." He broke down and cried, then left the church.

President Eisenhower displayed great interest in the development of the National Presbyterian Church and its building program. One night he gave a dinner for twenty or more Presbyterian laymen at the White House. He invited Henry Luce and me to present a plan for the new church. He asked us to give some indication of how our campaign for funds was coming along. During the evening the president urged the men present to rally around this program, to make their own gifts and seek gifts from other people. This dinner and the president's influence were effective in drawing strong support for the building program.

One Saturday morning the president phoned to talk to me about his own gift for the church. He indicated to me that he was directing Johnston and Lemon Company to send me certain stocks as his gift to the new church and center. His enthusiasm for the building of a symbolic and functional National Presbyterian Church in Washington never abated. Across the years he demonstrated his interest in the life of the church, even to serving as honorary chairman of the Presbyterian Fifty Million Dollar Campaign.

When the Eisenhowers became my parishioners, stories about the president's pastor appeared in newspapers and magazines across the country. Kenneth Dole wrote a six-column article for the front page of the Washington Post in which he said:

If a soldier president had hunted for a soldier pastor, Dr. Elson was the man for the post. His military carriage, his pink-and-white Legion of Merit button in his lapel, his activity in the General Commission on Chaplains, his advocacy of universal training, his spartan utterances, all reflect his soldierly cast of thought. A remarkable little book of his compositions written for distribution among the Armed Forces through the Korean

War provides for each day of the year a khaki-colored spiritual vitamin pill called *One Moment With God.* An impressive man in the pulpit, he gives discourses that are models of manly emphasis.

Similarly, Dr. Caspar Nannes published a cover article in *Collier's* magazine of November 11, 1955, under the caption, "The President and Pastor."

The president and his pastor look somewhat alike when they are together. Both stand ramrod straight, both have the same general facial contours and wispy, light-colored hair. The similarity does not end there. Like the president, Dr. Elson was raised in a home steeped in religious values, actively competed in and still enjoys athletics, and has known the discipline after discipline of military life. He conducts his office with such military precision that Catholic friends jokingly told him he was really a priest because "only a Jesuit would run his religious office with such discipline and thoroughness."

This thoroughness is still evident. It includes a fettish for being on time, as well as a militarylike inspection of the church choir on Sunday morning. The discipline extends also to his preaching. His sermons, rapped out in staccato tempo, are models of clarity, enunciation, and sentence structure, as well as content. A visitor of another denomination once listened to Dr. Elson deliver a nominating address for church moderator. The man said afterward, "If I ever run for office, I want Dr. Elson to do the nominating."

In fact, one year in our denomination, four candidates were announced for moderator of the General Assembly. By the time the General Assembly convened, each of the four had asked me to make his nominating speech.

The position of moderator of the General Assembly is the highest elective office one can hold in the Presbyterian Church. The moderator presides over the General Assembly and is the titular head of the Presbyterian Church.

In 1956 I was nominated for this post. I was in the Middle East at the time, but a committee was organized to present my candidacy throughout the church. Upon returning from my trip, I had to decide if I wished my candidacy to proceed. After discussing the matter with certain church leaders, I chose to allow the effort to proceed to its conclusion, whatever that might be.

What my supporters had not reckoned with was the fact that this was an election year, and I was publically perceived to be very close to the president of the United States. In this case, such good references worked against me. Voters reasoned that it might not be wise to elect as moderator the pastor of the president.

Another explanation was advanced. Two years before, Billy Graham had approached me with an idea for a new Christian magazine, one that would publish scholarly features, carry news of the Christian world, and be staffed by professional journalists. As an author contributing to many publications, Graham wanted my reaction to the idea, and I supported it. Editorial policies for some of the existing periodicals had become stale and predictable. I saw value in a publication that would be fresh, professional, and likely to be read widely. Thus I helped launch *Christianity Today* magazine.

Early in 1956 a press release was distributed announcing the new periodical. I was listed as a contributing editor. J. Howard Pugh, a financial supporter of *Christianity Today*, was known for his strong opposition to the National Council of Churches. Pugh's connection to the magazine on whose masthead I was listed caused me flack when the General Assembly convened later that year.

Just before the election of moderator, Dr. Paul Calvin Payne, my long-time friend and secretary of the Board of Christian Education, accosted me in the lobby of the hotel, shook his finger at me, and said, "This is an evil thing you and J. Howard Pugh are doing—starting a magazine to destroy the National Council of Churches!" I had in fact, as a Presbyterian delegate at its founding, strongly supported the National Council of Churches, but Payne insisted that my stature and Pugh's wealth had started something that would be gravely injurious to the NCC.

Losing the election for moderator had one great benefit. After this experience of defeat, I gained great empathy for many of my Washington parishioners whose careers rested on the winning or losing of elections.

SIX
THE PRESIDENT
AND HIS PASTOR

In the 1950s America experienced one of its great religious awakenings. This was reflected by Protestants, Catholics, Eastern Orthodox, Jews, Muslims, and others. Church membership expanded, new churches, synagogues, mosques, and tabernacles were being built. There were vital laymen's movements across every denomination. Divinity schools were crowded with promising clergy candidates. For the most part, they were veterans of World War II—war-conditioned, serious-minded, mature, deeply dedicated.

Infused with missionary zeal, women's societies flourished. Religious book markets boomed. Bible publishing expanded. Church periodicals prospered. Secular magazines invariably carried religious articles and, in the press, religious news moved from the church page to the front page. Moreover, mass evangelism reappeared, accenting such personalities as Billy Graham. Television was coming into its own with effective religious programs. Religious life once again became the norm for America, and for most of that decade the president led the way with his personal faith and life of prayer.

It may turn out in the long run of history that the exemplary practice of his Christian faith was Eisenhower's most enduring contribution to his times. Dwight Eisenhower was a genuinely good person. Nothing in him was synthetic or hypocritical. He was a man of sensitivity, firmness, infectious good humor, and a transparent sincerity not always seen in public life.

He dealt fairly with those who criticized his religious practice. Senator Neely of West Virginia, a Presbyterian layman, taunted him in press and in speech, but President Eisenhower seemed impervious to it. His life needed no defense. Critical observers referred sometimes to what they called his emphasis on "religion in general." This was his way of expressing the spiritual roots of all Americans. The fact is he was a devout member of the Presbyterian Church. He knew the church's standards, practices, and current leaders. He was committed to and upheld the doctrines of his church. Although he frequently differed with church pronouncements on civil affairs and foreign policy, his loyalties remained steadfast.

In speaking to the public as president of all the people, he was careful—as every president should be—to use universal, multidenominational language to speak of the abiding faith of Americans and the theistic basis of many American institutions. Every wise president speaks of religion and faith in God in inclusive terminology, assuring the world that faith in the transcendent God is the public philosophy that produces the social and civic atmosphere of America.

In Kansas City to deliver an address at a conference of Christian homemakers, I strolled out for exercise. I was startled to come upon an entire window in a big department store with my picture in it, beneath which were the words, "The president has a pastor—have you?" In the six-month period before Eisenhower professed his faith and joined the church, Billy Graham had three conferences with him at the Commodore Hotel in New York City, dealing with the president's personal spiritual life and his prior experience with churches and preachers. To Graham, the president-elect seemed to crave a spiritual home. He commended to General Eisenhower membership in the National Presbyterian Church, especially since Mrs. Eisenhower was already a Presbyterian. In a letter to me on January 19, 1953, Graham wrote me:

. . . I do not know of anybody in the entire world that could help him like you can. As I have thought about it and prayed about it, I am absolutely certain that God has placed you in this place of responsibility in being a spiritual helper to this man. . . .

I am certain your sermons, your prayers, your times alone with him will have much to do in influencing world history. You may rest assured that I have been in continual prayer that God will lead you, fill you, and anoint you for the tremendous task that lies ahead.

As the president and his wife were coming to a decision in that crucial week before February 1, 1953, I asked two men, Billy Graham and Harrison Ray Anderson, confidentially to be much in prayer for me and the Eisenhowers.

A year later, on Flag Day, February 14, 1954, Eisenhower stood on the east steps of the United States Capitol and, for the first time, asked his fellow Americans to join him in reciting the revised Pledge of Allegiance to the flag of the United States. He had just signed into law the legislation which included the words "under God" in the pledge. The two houses of Congress had adopted the bill which had been introduced in the Senate by Senator Homer Ferguson, a ruling elder of the National Presbyterian Church. This phrase symbolized the undergirding reality of Eisenhower's life. To be "under God" was the essence of his personal life and his constant prayer for the republic and for the world.

Looking back, it is clear that with the passing of each week, the pastor-parishioner relationship intensified.

On September 24, 1955, while the president was in Denver, he was suddenly seized by a severe heart attack. Mrs. Eisenhower called Dr. Snyder, the president's physician, who spent the night by the president's bed and early in the morning took the president to the hospital. The first twelve to forty-eight hours were critical. At first it did not seem expedient to give details of the president's seizure, but in a few hours, Mr. Murray Snyder, the assistant press secretary, released statements to the media that kept

Americans informed on the state of the president's health.

The president was immensely popular throughout the country. He was just what the country seemed to need and want in those postwar years. Consequently, the news of failing health alarmed the nation. People assembled in churches to pray for the president's recovery and for wisdom and skill for his doctors. The news of the president's illness came on a weekend, and in our church service that Sunday we had a special prayer for the president's recovery and for God's care of his wife and family.

Although the president was in Denver, the press was in our church in force on that day. When the service ended, the three main networks asked if I would offer a prayer for the president to be transmitted throughout the country over television. This I did, and by bedtime that night all Americans who believed joined in earnest prayer for their president and his family.

In the days that followed, I recorded on tape several carefully selected passages from the Psalms and the New Testament and sent them to the president in Denver. We also sent recordings of some of his favorite music as an inspiration to him.

Experts in cardiology across the country converged on Fitzsimmons Hospital, and after some anxious days the president began to show some steady improvement. A little later he resumed his painting. One of his finest paintings, in fact, is a snow scene that he did at the hospital while convalescing. He returned to Gettysburg on or about November 11. Shortly thereafter he and Mrs. Eisenhower invited Mrs. Elson and me to lunch for the dedication of the Gettysburg farmhouse.

The president's second illness occurred on June 8, 1956. I had participated in the FBI Academy graduation that morning and had remained for lunch in J. Edgar Hoover's quarters. There we were joined by Chief Justice Earl Warren, Assistant Attorney General Warren E. Burger, Herbert Brownell, William Rogers, and one or two others. As dessert was served, an assistant of Mr. Hoover entered and handed him the text of a telegram just received. Mr. Hoover read the message aloud. It reported that an ambulance was taking the president from the White House to Walter Reed Hospital.

Eisenhower had suffered serious stomach problems for years, but this time the pain was severe. The previously undiagnosed illness was ileitis, a young man's disease, which was why it had not been suspected. The president was informed that it was necessary for him to undergo a serious operation immediately. He indicated his approval, and between 3:00 and 5:00 A.M. a successful operation was performed.

There was, of course, great concern among his family, staff, and officials of the government. After his recovery he said that for him it was somewhat like his experience with the Battle of the Bulge. "I didn't get frightened until three weeks after it had begun, when I began to read the American papers and found how near we were to being whipped." Soon the president was well, back on the job, and resuming his golf and fishing.

The third illness during Eisenhower's presidency came on November 25, 1957, when he had a slight stroke. It was detected early by his devoted, gracious, and efficient secretary, Anne Whitman, who noticed that his words came out twisted. Given proper care, the president rapidly regained his powers of speech. He even came to church on Thanksgiving Day.

During each of his illnesses, I called upon him in the hospital and at home. After his retirement he returned to Walter Reed Hospital for short periods of treatment. On each of these occasions I visited him in the presidential suite. During his last illness, I visited regularly with members of the family, especially Mrs. Eisenhower, who was under severe strain. These later illnesses made an earlier experience in the Gettysburg house especially profound.

When the president had been released from Fitzsimmons Army Hospital following his first heart attack, he and Mrs. Eisenhower returned to their Gettysburg farmhouse for his convalescence, where he resumed in a limited way the duties of his office. From time to time the president and First Lady had spoken to me about their desire to dedicate this home with a religious service, and thus they invited us to be their guests on the day after Thanksgiving in 1955.

This was our first visit to the Eisenhowers' country home. It was about eleven o'clock when we reached the house and were graciously received at the front door by Mrs. Eisenhower, and shortly afterwards, by the president. We were settled comfortably in a glassed-in porch looking out upon a putting green. In the distance were the rolling pasturelands and the blue heights of Big Round Top. Major John Eisenhower and his wife, Barbara, joined us with Barbara's sister, Mary Thompson. Grandchildren made intermittent appearances.

Later, at lunch, the conversation turned upon church affairs and current events. The president spoke with gratitude about the many messages that had come to him from all over the world—messages of hope and encouragement and assurances of prayer from people of many faiths. The mood at the table was free and happy.

When lunch ended, everyone moved into a commodious drawing room, beautifully furnished with mementos from all parts of the world in which the president had served. When we were all comfortably settled, the president arose, walked toward the open fireplace, assumed a "parade rest" stance with his feet comfortably separated, and then began talking earnestly. He related how both he and Mrs. Eisenhower had been reared in a home with daily Bible reading and family prayers. They had lived in many dwellings in their long association with the army. But this was their first home, and they wanted to dedicate it to God.

I replaced the president in front of the fireplace and began the service with a call to worship: "Behold I stand at the door and knock; if any man hear my voice and open the door, I will come in." Then we read the familiar Psalm 23, followed by New Testament passages John 3:34, 35 and 1 Corinthians 13:4-7.

I quoted from Helen Taylor's familiar song, "Bless This House":

Bless this house, oh Lord we pray;
Make it safe by night and day.
Bless these walls so firm and stout,
Keeping want and trouble out. . . .

Bless this door that it may prove
Ever open to joy and love. . . .

Bless the folk who dwell within,
Keep them pure and free from sin.
Bless us all that we may be
Fit, oh Lord, to dwell with Thee.

Then I offered a prayer:

Eternal God whom we know as our Father, as Thou hast accompanied these Thy servants in many dwelling places, through manifold services in the uttermost parts of the earth, accept now we beseech Thee, the dedication of this house that it may henceforth be a place of health and healing, a haven of tranquility, an abode of love and a sanctuary of worship. Bless all who name it home and all the loved ones and friends who are encompassed by an abiding love and devotion to Thee.

Here may hallowed memories and sacred recollections be called forth. Here may Thy servants know the gratitude of all the people of this nation. Here may Thy name be honored. Here may there ever be a witness to Thy grace and truth, that goodness and mercy follow these, Thy servants, all their days that they may abide in Thy house forever. Through Jesus Christ, our Lord. Amen.

Following this prayer, we all joined in the Lord's Prayer, and the brief service was concluded by the benediction:

The Lord bless you and keep you.
The Lord make His face to shine upon you

139

and be gracious unto you.
The Lord lift up his countenance upon you
and give you peace. Amen.

There was something unforgettable and profoundly moving about this brief service—not only because it was the president of the United States with his family worshiping in his own home after the anxiety of a serious illness, but because this was a good Christian family and an exemplary American household. There was no news story from the White House about this event, and that was the way it should be—and the way the president wished it. This was a family and a pastoral affair.

Many times since that day, when encouraging newly married couples to make their home a place of worship, I have thought of this home and its high dedication. I remember that when I said, "Let us pray," the president's grandchildren, Dwight David, Barbara Anne, and Susan Elaine, spontaneously knelt down at a low black lacquered table. This was the American home at its best. How many times I have prayed since then that this could be a character of all American homes. The principal religious celebrations of the ancient Jews took place in the home. Like the ancient Jewish faith, Christianity has been a faith for the family.

In early America, home was a sanctuary of worship; the father was the priest of his own household; the open Bible was the sourcebook for Christian worship, the textbook for his education, and the inspiration for the establishment of his political institutions. We have not outlived the need for the open Book, for the message of God in and through the family, and for the spiritual discipline of prayer. Perhaps we would be better people now if the home were still honored as a sanctuary of worship.

For a great historical event we were to be in the Eisenhower home in Scotland. In October 1960 the Church of Scotland was celebrating its 400th anniversary of the Reformation. Helen and I were planning to be present. When the president learned that we were going to the General Assembly in Edinburgh, he invited me to the Oval Office for a visit.

The president indicated that he would like to send a message to the General Assembly of the Church of Scotland if that were deemed appropriate. I assured him that I thought any message from the president of the United States, especially our highly honored wartime military leader, would be welcomed by the people of Scotland. In the course of our conversation, the president turned to me and said, "How would you and Helen like to live in Culzean Castle while you're visiting Scotland?" This castle had been given to the Eisenhowers to use for as long as either of them lived. I happily assured him that it would be a joy for us to stay in his castle.

In a day or two a courier brought the presidential message to my office. Meanwhile, the Presbyterian women of the United States had been developing a gift for the women of the Church of Scotland on this historic occasion. A Presbyterian minister carved for the women a Celtic cross of American balsam wood that was nine feet tall. We carried this huge cross proudly but, I confess, not easily.

141

The time came when the program of the General Assembly got under way. Her Majesty Queen Elizabeth said that it was the first time the reigning monarch had been back to observe the proceedings of the General Assembly in several hundred years.

The moderator, the Right Reverend J. H. S. Burleigh, and the clerks of the General Assembly knew that I carried a message from the president, but this had not been announced in the program or in the press. Consequently, the Scottish *Daily Mail* for Wednesday, October 12, 1960, reported:

The complete surprise of the Assembly belonged, not to the queen or the moderator, but to President Eisenhower. Without a hint to anybody of his intentions, he sent his own minister to Edinburgh with a personal message of greeting to the kirk.

Up to the lectern stepped Dr. Elson, the minister of the National Presbyterian Church in Washington, the church where the president worships every Sunday. "He has the best church-going record of any president of the United States in this century," Dr. Elson told me. The president not only sent Dr. Elson to Edinburgh with a message, but he gave him his keys to Culzean Castle, Ayrshire, so that he could stay there during his visit to Scotland.

The president's message which Dr. Elson read was: "I welcome this opportunity to acknowledge my nation's indebtedness to the spiritual and intellectual resources of Scotland. A symbol of this indebtedness, the Reverend Dr. John Witherspoon, stands outside the door of our church in Washington.

"Born near Edinburgh and nurtured in the land of his fathers, Witherspoon became a heroic leader of Americans in their struggle for independence. As such, he represents the great hosts of Scots who helped to build my country and whose

142

descendants give living strength to the bonds which unite our peoples.

"In grateful acknowledgement of our common heritage, I send my best wishes to the members and guests of the General Assembly."

In Scotland, Eisenhower was tremendously popular. The commissioners at the General Assembly immediately stood and stomped their feet in great exhilaration at the greeting from the one American whose affections they most cherished.

The big day for the women came when Her Majesty Queen Elizabeth visited their convocation. Another Edinburgh newspaper, *The Scotsman*, began its story by saying:

The queen placed another seal upon the affection in which she is held by her Scottish subjects yesterday afternoon when, as the first sovereign to come to the General Assembly of the Church of Scotland since 1602, she addressed the fathers and brethren of the kirk. It was one of the most brilliant scenes ever witnessed in the Assembly Hall, fittingly crowning the Hall's 100th year.

In this profound and historic ceremony, Helen presented on behalf of the Presbyterian women of America the beautiful, handcrafted Celtic cross. The cross was accepted for the women of the Church of Scotland by the president of the Women's Association. Now it rests in the chapel at the headquarters of the church in Edinburgh, where it is a daily inspiration for those who work there.

We regard this experience as one of the high moments in our lives and, indeed, in the life of the two churches: the one in Scotland and the other in America, which owes

143

such a debt to the Church of Scotland for the leaders who came to this country in the days of our founding.

I will never forget the conclusion of Queen Elizabeth's address to the General Assembly:

The lesson from the Reformation is one that all Christians may surely apply to the modern world. If we have faith and courage to seek it, we shall be shown new truth in the gospel of real and immediate relevance to our own time, and we shall be given new insight to understand the unexampled problems which arise almost every day at home and abroad.

As one who loves this country of Scotland and her people, I rejoice that it is a mark of her national church to combine devotion to the unalterable Christian faith with an eagerness to find new truth to answer the needs of a changing world.

The General Assembly concluded its lofty expressions and we resumed our journey. The impact of it all was to send me back to Washington more concerned than ever that the National Presbyterian Church be a place in which ceremonial moments of historical significance could be accomplished. Washington needs a symbolic and functional church that says to the world, "Here is the meaning of the witness of the Presbyterian Church."

By the way, we did enjoy the accommodations at the castle.

Another high event of the Eisenhower years in the White House also involved Queen Elizabeth. She and Prince Philip, Duke of Edinburgh, were invited to attend the National Presbyterian Church on Sunday, October 20, 1957. The president showed great personal concern that the church service be conducted as it would on any ordinary Sunday. It was not to be uniquely developed around the presence of the queen—but in the end we did make some alterations for the guests of honor.

One of the troublesome aspects was the final confirmation that Her Majesty and Prince Philip would attend the church service with the president on this date. There was great hesitation on the part of the Commonwealth ambassadors who formed the committee on the queen's visit to give a firm answer to the president's invitation. Secretary of State John Foster Dulles and members of the White House staff attempted to get a firm reply about the queen's program for this Sunday. Finally, the president said one day to a staff aide, "Get the British ambassador on the telephone for me."

"We seem to be having difficulty getting a firm acceptance of Her Majesty's invitation for Sunday church with me and Mrs. Eisenhower," said the president to the ambassador. "When I'm in her country and her guest, I go to her church. When she is in my country and my guest, we go to my church."

At that moment the queen's proposed attendance at the service on October 20 was confirmed and the plans went forward without obstruction. Some days before the Sunday service, the president asked me to come to the Oval Office to discuss the matter. First he wanted to know if we had selected the hymns, to which I said we had some hymns selected, but they were subject to substitution or change. So he asked, "How would it be if we sang as a processional hymn, 'Holy, Holy, Holy'?"

"Mr. President," I replied, "that's exactly the hymn we had tentatively put down, and we had also put down the hymn with which we closed your preinaugural service, 'God of Our Life Through All the Circling Years.' For the recessional we suggest the old hymn, 'Our God, Our Help in Ages Past,' to the tune of St. Anne."

The president said, "That's just a wonderful way to leave a church service."

"Mr. President," I ventured, "it seems to me that with the queen in attendance we ought to have something from the Scottish Psalter just before the sermon. What would you think of our singing 'The Lord Is My Shepherd' to the Crimmond tune?"

"That's a fine selection, and it's a very singable tune." Then he surprised me. "I have a special request I would like to make. After the offering we usually stand to sing the Doxology, hear the offertory prayer, and sing 'Our Fathers' God to Thee.' At that point I wonder if the choir would be willing to sing in tribute to Her Majesty, the hymn 'God Save the Queen.'"

Jim Haggarty, the president's press secretary, who was the only other person present in this conference, spoke up. "Mr. President, the people in Protocol tell us that we should never render the national anthem of another nation unless it is immediately followed by the rendering of our own national anthem, 'The Star Spangled Banner.'"

In a flash the president leaned across his desk, looked at both Haggarty and me, and said, "I know they say that in Protocol, but where I am, I make the protocol. So, Dr. Elson, if you have no objection and the choir is willing, I would be grateful if the choir would sing 'God Save the Queen' without our national anthem."

When we had covered other items and I rose to leave, I spoke to the president about the sermon. I had been preaching a series of sermons on the Beatitudes, and if I preached the sermon that was scheduled and that was already prepared in text form, the text for the Sunday of the queen's service would be "Blessed are the meek for they shall inherit the earth." I said, "Mr. President, I'm a little concerned about what cynical columnists and the media might do in reflecting on the text of the sermon if I proceed to preach the sermon I have prepared. I have been wondering if it might not be more appropriate and inspiring for us if I could deliver a sermon on peace, using the Beatitude "Blessed are the peacemakers for they shall be called the children of God."

The president scowled at the thought of even considering a change in the sermon subject just because of the hazard of misuse by the media. But after some thoughtful silence, the president flashed his big Eisenhower grin and said, "Well, Dr. Elson, the more I think about it, the more I think it might be more helpful if Her Majesty and I could be associated with a sermon on peacemaking rather than something on the meek. The British are not inheriting much of the earth these days."

Accordingly, despite many appointments in those five or six days before the queen's visit I did what one does in college before exams. I crammed. Meanwhile, the physical arrangements for a high day such as this were necessarily elaborate. The instructions, which accompanied cards to our special guests, covered three pages. On Saturday night before Her Majesty was to come to the church service, we found ourselves in a musical predicament. Dr. Theodore Schaefer, our distinguished organist and choirmaster, was also the accompanist of the famed soprano Mildred Miller. They were presenting a Saturday night concert in Miami, Florida, and expected to be back sometime after midnight on the last flight from Miami to Washington.

Misfortune of misfortunes—the plane broke down in Miami! Secret Service officers were frantically trying to find ways to get our organist to the church for the historic service the next morning. Intermittently during the night and morning we were getting reports of the repairs to the airplane and the prospect of Dr. Schaefer getting back on time.

Finally the plane was repaired, but it arrived in Washington sometime after the eleven o'clock service had begun. Dr. Schaefer was rushed by police to the National Presbyterian Church, where he arrived in time to play the recessional hymn and postlude.

Our trepidation need not have been as great as it was, for Marlene Baver, the assistant organist, played superbly and directed the choir and the singing of "God Save the Queen." Sometimes it's the little things that test a man's religion.

In any case, the coming of the queen with the president to the National Presbyterian Church will long remain a treasured event. What was so significant for the ministers and officers of the church was that, despite the complicated and elaborate arrangements, when the service began we were liberated from all anxiety and worry and concentrated on conducting the service and lifting our vision upward.

My sermon, "The Way of Peacemakers," suited the occasion and evoked a wide response from those who were present and from the world at large when it was reported through the press and media. I was further encouraged when this sermon was the only sermon included in that year's annual book of great addresses published by the University of Louisiana.

I was greatly touched the day after the church service when an officer of the queen's staff asked to see me in my study. He came with all the polish and dignity of a member of the queen's court and presented me with a package. I promptly opened it to find an autographed photograph of Her Majesty and the prince in civilian attire with two of their small children, Charles and Anne, in the garden at one of their homes. This photograph with the queen's autograph now hangs on the wall of my study at the Westchester in Washington.

That picture rests just below one of the young, dashing King Hussein.

All my adult life I have been a student of the Middle East and much traveled in that part of the world. For 150 years the Presbyterian Church, in cooperation with other denominations, had been at work in the Middle East through missionaries, educators, medical personnel, and evangelists. The first woman physician to go to the Middle East from America was Dr. Mary Eddy, sent and supported by the women of what is now the National Presbyterian Church.

For many years I made regular visits to the Middle East and was chairman of the National Council of the American Friends of the Middle East, lecturing in colleges, universities, and theological institutions in most of the countries of that part of the world. Although much of my itinerary took me to the Middle East offices of the American Friends of the Middle East, I made regular visits to Israel where I saw Prime Minister Ben-Gurion, Golda Meir, Joseph Herzog, and others.

I remember Ben-Gurion patting his Bible, talking about military campaigns in the Old Testament, reveling in the brilliance of Joshua's march against Jericho. It seemed to me that his affection for the Bible was not so much based on love for the Word of God as on its value as a textbook of military strategies.

In Jordan I saw King Hussein on a regular basis when he was a very young king, and I saw his cousin King Faisal before his assassination. In fact, one of my published lectures was dedicated to King Faisal. In Syria I saw Prime Minister Kuwatly, and in Egypt I was twice alone with President Nasser in his home. I met many Christian clergymen and educators and a great many Muslim leaders, and I spoke at the Alazar, the oldest theological seminary in the world. I became well acquainted with our American foreign service officers who specialized in Middle East affairs.

Under the Eisenhower Doctrine, President Eisenhower

had sent a military force of some eight thousand personnel into Lebanon. Knowing my lifelong travel, study, and concern for the Middle East, Eisenhower asked me for a memorandum suggesting how to speak and what to say when he addressed the General Assembly of the United Nations. I prepared my remarks on Sunday, July 24, 1958, despite many interruptions throughout the busy day. I delivered my paper at the White House as our family was departing in our station wagon for our home in Nova Scotia where we would spend the summer. Among other things I said:

. . . The Middle East people are inexperienced in democratic processes. They build life around strong personalities. You have your own personal prestige and the residual resources in American friendship on which to build in this time of crisis. . . .

The people of the Middle East will understand us if we communicate in spiritual terms. It will help to acknowledge our indebtedness to the Middle East for contributing to the world the three great religions of Semitic origin. We must find a way to identify ourselves with the Arab's cultural aspirations for freedom under God, for self-fulfillment and the achievement of an honorable national destiny consonant with their cultural and religious heritage. . . .

It is important to do the right thing. It is of equal importance to say the right thing and to say it now. Here are some things which could be said: Assure the Middle East peoples of our abiding friendship. We are remembered for our educators, doctors, nurses, philanthropists, and missionaries. Although the tactical necessities of diplomacy have hurt them, there remains a deep people-to-people friendship. Assure them that it is still there. . . .

Pledge to the Middle East peoples our determination to work

through the United Nations and with our own resources to improve the life of all peoples in the area. When the situation stabilizes we ought to help solve the problems incident to the partition of Palestine, the anguished refugees, the Holy City, and indeed, the whole future of Palestine. . . .

It is not too late to be to them again what once we were—their ideal and pattern for all life. . . .

When we arrived in our lovely community on Cape Breton Island, there was in my box at the post office a two-page, single spaced letter from the president, saying:

July 28, 1958

Dear Dr. Elson:

Jim Haggarty reported to me his interesting conversation with you and gave me the fine memorandum you prepared with suggestions as to how we might best deal with the Middle East. I value your ideas, particularly because of your long experience and interest in the Middle East. There is little indeed in what you have to say with which I disagree. I am greatly impressed by your beliefs as to the relations we should maintain with the Arabs as people.

Then the president went on to say that I did not mention one very complicated factor:

I refer to the obviously unbridled ambition of Nasser—an ambition that seems to compel him to seek one political success after another. As I see him he wants only public acclaim at any cost, even though the cost must be paid by the people he pretends to serve.

My thanks for giving me the benefit of your thoughts on this complicated problem and warm personal regards.

Before I had a chance to acknowledge this letter, another letter arrived from the White House. It took me some time to absorb what the president was writing:

July 31, 1958

Personal

Dear Dr. Elson:

Since my first note to you on the subject, I have been pondering carefully the interesting letter you left with Jim Haggarty. Because of the earnest thought you have devoted to Mid-East problems and your personal acquaintance with the region, I am stealing the time to write you again at greater length than normally I could do. Even so, I can do no more than to set out in random fashion a few factors of the problems. . . .

There is an old military saying that "nothing positive can be accomplished except from a strong base." So our position of strength must comprise not only the necessary military force in critical spots with proper support and reserves behind it, but the United States must itself be a strong base, out of which positive action can be projected if necessary.

I want to pursue this thought a moment. The real strength of America must be described in values that are intangible. It is a truism to say that the strength of democracy is public opinion. When there is a truly unified public opinion, there is a tremendous power generated by our free people. Further, when that public opinion is based upon knowledge and real understanding of the issues involved, then this tremendous power can produce and sustain constructive action almost without limit.

By and large, you are well aware of the basic purposes, hopes, and efforts of the American government in the foreign field. Those efforts in the Middle East are based on convictions that largely parallel your own. Yet I feel that all of us must do more here at home if we are to be successful abroad. I have made some speeches on this subject, three or four of them on nationwide television. But I believe teachers, business leaders, labor leaders, and especially the clergy ought to be active in this work.

If all of us are to be active and effective, it must be on the basis that we have studied the problems realistically; our purposes must be lofty; and we must demand from ourselves a full measure of dedication to the principles that have inspired this nation in the great moments of its history. We may and probably should be emotional and sentimental in the proper sense, but we must come right down to earth if our conclusions are to be realistic and our efforts productive. . . .

We must be true to our religious heritage, recognizing clearly the basic principles by which we must attempt to guide our nation's destiny. But we must not fail to recognize that it is humans who must make temporal decisions. If those decisions are to conform to fundamental convictions and be logical and timely, there must be earnest and deep study and contemplation, not only by officials, but by the people who produce the power through which such important projects are implemented. The phrase "Will to greatness" is an expression of a noble ideal. It will be achieved only if all of us—leaders and followers, each in his own sphere—uses his heart, his brain, and his body to make it so.

With warm regards,
D. E.

One cannot help but be deeply touched by the president's brilliant mind and his substantive discussion of the forces at work in our world and the difficulty of dealing with the situation in the Middle East.

On August 4 I replied to the letters the president had sent to me at our summer home:

Your two letters commenting on my recent Middle East summary and my conversation with Mr. Haggarty have reached me here, and I am gratified that some of the ideas are suggestive to you. I am especially appreciative of your second, more detailed commentary, the last two paragraphs of which form one of the noblest American expressions to appear at any time in our history.

Your letter prompts me to send an additional commentary. About Nasser: I did not elaborate on this complicated factor. Instead, I checked the two sentences on page 3 and asked Mr. Haggarty to indicate what I was driving at. One year ago, August 9, 1957, I reported to you that the most disappointing aspect of my interview of 1½ hours alone with Nasser was his total disregard of and lack of appreciation for your action in the Sinai-Suez crisis of October-November 1954. He took all the credit for ending the conflict and told the people so. To me, he said it was the Egyptian strategic withdrawal from Sinai, the army, and the civilian population which created a firm unity. Government, army, and people, and the prospect of volunteers from abroad brought the end of the operations.

I was disappointed, shocked, and somewhat frightened by the way he handled the facts of history. He began as a young idealist and now dashes capriciously from one expediency to another in order to remain in power. Nasser's actions are better understood in the light of his three great humiliations, and we should remember the conditioning of leaders when we assess what they are saying in their public documents. First, he has the boyhood memory of Egyptian social structure. The king and wealthy landholders at the top and the poor villagers at the bottom. Two, the memory of colonial rulership. Three, two successive military defeats at the hands of the "upstart" Israeli army. He's a soldier and it hurts all the more. He overcompensated for these lurking memories.

This does not make him any better but helps us understand

him. Nasser as a person is one person. Nasser as a symptom or symbol is another problem. This is what makes it so complicated and downright aggravating. Discouraging as present developments are, the enormous prestige of Nasser prompted my brief comment, "Guide from within." Take a chance on real neutrality. Deal in the open with Nasser and whoever is the real symbol of national unity. . . .

The alternative to Nasser, I said, would be a bloodbath and turbulence throughout the Middle East, possibly lasting for a long, long time. Continuing my comment, I said, we need a better understanding of the Middle East by Americans to secure ample public support for Eisenhower's policies:

For years some of us have been working at this job and have developed through American Friends of the Middle East the most effective instrument for promoting friendship on both sides. I am chairman of the National Council, and the board members are men of national eminence who are your friends.

Your thesis about American strength resting upon intangible values reveals to me your fundamental philosophy at its best. Here the clergy can be helpful. Too many churchmen are too negative in their attitude toward government, but it is also true that the main support for the mutual security program has been the church, its press, and spokesmen. The church can be expected to give even greater encouragement to such programs because the programs are right.

In my sermon "Freedom Is Not Free," preached on May 25, which Mr. Dulles later discussed with you, I said the great agony of the Christian statesman turns on the proper use of great power for moral ends. That you seek to discover the will of God in your vocation is clearly revealed in this exchange of notes.

God's blessing be upon you, Mr. President, in the coming days. Command me for any service I may render.

Our communications on the Middle East were not always so serious. For many years the small group of Christians on duty at the several embassies in Kabul, Afghanistan, were maintaining a church congregation in this capital city in a country which tolerated only the faith of Islam. The Reverend Christy Wilson, Jr., and his church officers had repeatedly petitioned the government for permission to build a small church. Just as often the request was denied. On the Sunday before President Eisenhower left Washington for a state visit to several Middle Eastern and Asian countries, I told him I had been in Egypt at the time the new mosque was dedicated in Washington and that the press there carried vivid photos of the president and First Lady removing their shoes as they entered the Washington mosque to participate in its dedication. "This made a tremendous hit throughout the Muslim world. Washington has its mosque, but Kabul has no Christian church."

The president saw at once his opportunity to help, and he seized it. "I will have only four hours in Kabul, and will of course, be with His Majesty the king," he said. "If a discreet moment occurs, I shall mention the desirability of a church in Kabul, especially since we accent freedom of religion in America."

Soon the Reverend Christy Wilson had his permit and built a simple church without a cross on its steeple, the only restriction remaining. (Unhappily, at a later period during an outbreak of violent fanaticism, the church building was bulldozed out of existence.)

Recent policy toward the Middle East has not changed much. Today's problems stem from the decision in 1948 to partition Palestine.

One problem today, a situation we don't like to address, is that the nation of Israel cannot support itself without the financial and military aid of the United States. Another part of the problem is our misunderstanding of the culture. Part of the mentality of the Arab is the ingrained cultural idea that land is not real estate to be traded, bought, sold, but rather an extension of the personality of the individual. The land and the person are one and the same thing.

Some American Christians today, following what they perceive to be the direction of biblical prophecy, seem to have a one-sided perspective of Middle East affairs. They are ignorant of Arab culture and thought. And in their allegiance to the state of Israel they fail to support their brothers and sisters in the region—Palestinian and Arab Christians.

Despite contacts with Nasser and my growing knowledge of Arab concerns, I was not an official emmisary of the United States government but traveled to the Middle East as a private citizen interested in the religious affairs of that region. Though my opinions were often sought during the Truman and Eisenhower administrations, my comments and suggestions were solicited apart from official foreign policy.

Once, when I was again planning a visit to the Middle East, the trip was duly reported in Sunday morning's church bulletin. Imagine our surprise when on Monday morning a column by Marguerite Higgins in the *New York Herald Tribune* reported that President Eisenhower had asked "a distinguished American clergyman to explore the prospects of peace between the Israelis and Arabs." In subsequent articles the paper identified the clergyman as Edward L. R. Elson.

Apparently, the news in the church bulletin, coupled with my pastoral relationship with the president, caused the reporter to put two and two together to get five. Later, the president's press secretary, Jim Haggarty, issued a clarification that although the president was in church when the announcement of the trip was made, I was not an official emmisary of the United States government.

Once each year for a good many years of my Washington ministry, Dr. Haballah, the director of the Islamic Institute, invited me to give a lecture in which I interpreted to the Muslim community the religious forces at work in the United States. Because I was a pastor of the National Presbyterian Church and had traveled and lectured much in the Middle East, I always received a cordial and gracious reception.

159

One snowy winter night a surprisingly large audience appeared. Dr. Haballah had a number of announcements to make before presenting the speaker. One of the announcements was to the effect that the interior of the mosque could not be completed with its beautifully delicate tile because of a forty thousand dollar insufficiency of funds.

I completed my lecture and responded to questions. Dr. Haballah thanked me profusely. At this point in the meeting, Dr. Shabandar, a newly arrived ambassador, walked up to the front of the room and handed Dr. Haballah a check for forty thousand dollars. Dr. Haballah began to jump up and down, slapping me on the back and exclaiming, "Praise be to Allah! Dr. Elson, this is your forty thousand dollar lecture. Thank you, thank you."

As I left the building, Dr. Haballah accompanied me to my car, repeating over and over again, "This is your forty thousand dollar lecture. Praise be to Allah!" Work on the mosque was resumed.

Shortly after my "forty thousand dollar lecture" at the Islamic Institute, the National Presbyterian Church launched its annual stewardship campaign to underwrite its budget for the new year. I made a little report to my people, saying that I had given a lecture at the Islamic Institute of such power and persuasion that one man wrote out a check for forty thousand dollars for use by the mosque. "You Presbyterians hear me when I say that I have been preaching Sunday after Sunday for well on to fifteen years and no individual has walked up here after any sermon and handed in a forty thousand dollar check.

Take heed to the lesson from the Muslims. 'Go, thou, and do likewise.'"

My message found its mark. In the following years many times forty thousand dollars was forthcoming to completely underwrite the building of the new National Presbyterian Church and Center.

Sometimes getting a message across depends upon the power of the person receiving it. One Sunday morning I was escorting President Eisenhower to his limousine and our conversation turned to a number of brief topics. On reaching the sidewalk I remarked, "There are a lot of unhappy soldiers this week since the quartermaster general announced that the beautiful horses serving the Arlington Cemetery ceremonies would be retired at the end of the fiscal year."

That report touched a tender spot with the president, who was surprised and unhappy. He had not known that this national cemetery would no longer have the horse-drawn caisson for military funerals.

I alerted him to an extensive story in the papers that day, describing the use of horses in the army and outlining the quartermaster general's statements. As the president drove away, he said, "Thank you for calling my attention to the proposed retirement of the Arlington horses."

About the middle of the following week, a story appeared in the papers in which the quartermaster general had reversed his intention and announced that the horses would continue their time-honored function.

As Eisenhower came to the end of his administration, he determined to deliver his farewell address over radio and television on January 17, 1961, at 8:30 P.M. It was in this address that Eisenhower spoke the sentences that would thereafter be so frequently quoted:

A hostile ideology, global in scope, atheistic in character, ruthless in purpose, and insidious in method. The danger that it poses for the nation and for the world is of indefinite duration.

These memorable words had to do with the military-industrial complex and its possible influence upon American life. The sentences summed up his deepest feelings, gave voice to his deepest fears. They were the words of a general who had given his life to the defense of freedom and the achievement of peace.

This conjunction of an immense military establishment and a large arms industry is new in American experience. In the councils of government we must guard against the acquisition of unwarranted influence, whether sought or unsought, by the military-industrial complex. The potential for the disastrous rise of misplaced power exists and will persist. No such allignment should be allowed to cripple or impede the pure exercise of our democratic life.

In the news conference that followed this address, the president emphasized that his greatest disappointment was his failure to achieve peace. "I wish I could say tonight that a lasting peace is in sight." But the most he could say was that "war has been avoided," and he concluded his newscast by praying that "all peoples will come to live together in a peace guaranteed by the binding forces of mutual respect and love."

In a letter dated April 4, 1956, Eisenhower wrote to Richard L. Simon, president of Simon and Schuster:

We are rapidly getting to the point that no war can be won. War implies a contest. When you get to the point that contest is no longer involved, the outlook comes close to destruction of the enemy and suicide for ourselves—an outlook that neither side can ignore, then arguments as to the exact amount of available strength as compared to somebody else's are no longer vital issues.

When we get to the point, as we one day will, both sides know that in any outbreak of general hostilities, regardless of the element of surprise, destruction will be both reciprocal and complete, possibly we will have sense enough to meet at the conference table with the understanding that the era of armaments has ended and the human race must conform its actions unto this truth or die.

The fullness of this potentiality has not yet been attained and I do not, by any means, decry the need for strength. That strength must be spiritual, economic, and military. All three are important and they are not mutually exclusive. They are all part of and the product of the American genious, the American will.

This was the heart and soul of Eisenhower, coming all the way from his boyhood years in a simple Midwestern community of peace-loving River Brethren.

Following his farewell address, the Eisenhowers withdrew from the Washington scene to their Gettysburg farm where life would be different. The retired general of the army, now relaxed from the presidency, spent his time writing books, visiting with old friends, attending church, and now and then playing some golf or going fishing.

As the months passed into years, the president's health gradually failed. During his presidency he had survived several serious illnesses, but now he had to be mindful of his conduct on a daily basis. From time to time he was a patient in Walter Reed Hospital, and I made a point of visiting with him.

Meanwhile, the work of building the new National Presbyterian Church went on with devotion. A building committee, under the chairmanship of Major General Reginald Harmon, was organized and met frequently. Other committees worked to raise the necessary funds. The old property at Connecticut Avenue was sold, emptied, and (amid some controversy) demolished. The new National Presbyterian Church made use of all of the windows that once were in the old church, as well as the beautiful great chandelier, the pews of many presidents, and other items of historical significance.

The date for the unveiling of the cornerstone of the new church at 4100 Nebraska Avenue, N.W., was set for General Eisenhower's birthday, Saturday, October 14, 1967. He had consented to unveil the cornerstone. A great crowd of people gathered on the stone platform outside the church. General and Mrs. Eisenhower were met by General Harmon, myself, other officers of the church, and the moderator of the General Assembly.

The liturgy for the unveiling of the cornerstone was

simple and profoundly meaningful. When the ceremony concluded, hundreds of people assembled in the Mayflower Hotel to express appreciation for what the president had meant to the nation in his personal religious life. At the conclusion of the luncheon I had the privilege of making a brief statement:

When a president of the United States speaks of spiritual values and the theistic consensus on which our national life is erected, he must, by virtue of his being the president of all the people, speak in general and inclusive terms. In the public execution of his office, he is, of course, mindful of all religious faiths. But his own religious life and that of his family must be nourished by and lived out in a particular community of believers.

As the whole world now knows, General Eisenhower, you as the thirty-fourth president of the United States chose to make your community of faith the congregation that traces its origin to a company of Scottish stonemasons, who, while working on the construction of the White House, held services in a carpenter's shop in a thicket which is now part of the White House grounds. Since the days when they sang the songs from the Scottish hymnary, received the sacraments, and heard the Word of God in the carpenter's shop, this company of Christians has been in pilgrimage in our age to a cluster of buildings which will serve generations yet to come. The symbols of our heritage and the vitality of our witness will go with us.

I concluded by announcing that the new main chapel, named the "Chapel of the Presidents," would be dedicated in tribute to Eisenhower. The Chapel has a window portraying him signing the bill incorporating the words "under God" into the Pledge of Allegiance. It also has the pew occupied by the Eisenhowers.

165

The former president never attended the dedication of the Chapel of the Presidents, for his health continued to decline, and he spent extended periods of time hospitalized. But with the passing of time, Eisenhower seemed increasingly to be a source of spiritual strength and intellectual wisdom for all who came in touch with him.

I recall one time waiting in the outer reception room, expecting soon to see the former president, when out of his room came President Lyndon Johnson. President Johnson took me by the arm into a corner where we were in private and said, "You know, Dr. Elson, when I am in trouble and the burdens of the presidency seem unbearable, this is where I come. There is more distilled wisdom in that sick man's room than any other place in all of North America."

One night as the end of his life drew near, Eisenhower asked his nurse, Captain Karen Uhler, to read some favorite passages from the Bible and to play softly some recordings by the Amherst College Choir and the Mormon Tabernacle Choir.

Early the next morning, March 28, 1969, he died. It was determined by the family, the protocol officers, and others that the funeral would be held in the Washington Cathedral and that I would be assisted in the funeral service by the dean of the cathedral, the Very Reverend Francis Sayre, Jr., and by the Episcopal bishop of the diocese of Washington, Bishop Creighton.

At various intervals over several years, Dean Sayre and I had conferred about the service after having discussed it with members of the family and some friends. The Scripture selections were approved by the family; the hymns had the former president's blessing long before he died, as had the participants whom he had designated. We had planned what was to happen on each of the five days between the death and the funeral service.

Some items had been changed by the ailing leader or by his family as the date of death approached. The former president had substituted "A Mighty Fortress Is Our God" for "Battle Hymn of the Republic," and he added the haunting old West Point song he loved, "Army Blue."

Eisenhower had also seemed to be greatly inspired by the "Palms" by Fauré, which was sung each Palm Sunday by Katherine Hansel or George Barrett, soloists of the National Presbyterian Church choir. We assured the former president that this would be rendered at the proper time and place. It was as though he had been given a foreknowledge from heaven that his death would occur on the weekend of Palm Sunday, and the world would be listening to one of his favorite musical compositions, "The Palms."

The army band played "The Palms" as the cortege moved up the steps and into the rotunda where the body would lie in state. The former president had requested that the chaplain of the Senate offer the prayers in the Capitol. As it happened, a few weeks before the president's death, Dr. Frederick Brown Harris retired as senate chaplain, and I was elected. Thus I officiated both at the Capitol and in the cathedral.

The service was broadcast across the world over television and radio networks. When the day was over, representatives of the media told me that this service had been heard and seen by more people than any similar event in all human history.

When the funeral had ended, Helen and I went with the family to the railroad station to say good-bye to the Eisenhower family as they boarded the special train which would take them to Abilene, where the former president would be interred in the Place of Meditation.

Ten years later I conducted a small funeral service in the chapel at Fort Meyer for Mamie Doud Eisenhower, who had shared her husband's faith as she had his life.

Thus ended one of the great friendships of my life.

SEVEN
THE SENATE
AS A PARISH

On the first Sunday of the Kennedy administration, President and Mrs. Kennedy attended mass in St. Matthews Cathedral on Rhode Island Avenue. At this time, St. Matthews and National Presbyterian both opened onto a court at the rear, so their back doors were face to face.

This Sunday the policemen, firemen, and Secret Service, who had been at our church every Sunday for eight years during the Eisenhower administration, were now protecting the president in the cathedral.

Our church services went according to schedule, but we missed the presence of the president and his entourage. That, however, was not our only loss that morning. Later, when I walked to my private rooms to be divested, what should I behold but the vestry in total disorder, ransacked and burglarized. This, of course, while the Secret Service was around the corner in St. Matthews.

I knew all the Kennedy brothers in one way or another. They were political colleagues of my brother Roy. Several of them helped him in his political campaigns, and he helped them in return. I also knew their mother, Mrs. Rose Kennedy. An invitation to offer prayers at Rose Kennedy's birthday party gave me an opportunity to enjoy a visit of substance with this remarkable matriarch of the Kennedy home.

President John Kennedy, one of the most eloquent speakers that America has produced, was a superb representative of a new generation and a leader at an early age. He had the capacity to select good assistants and the resources with which to compensate them properly. He possessed a precise mind and knew how to organize his thoughts. When he spoke, his message was transmitted through an attractive and winsome personality.

His brother Robert was a hard worker and, of the three Kennedys I have known, generally the most ruthless in his politics; a man of single purpose who did what he felt was necessary to fulfill the goal to which he happened to be committed at a particular period in his life.

He was bright, which helped to mitigate his lack of experience in the legal profession when he was made attorney general.

I shall never forget the night at the Alfalfa Club immediately following the Kennedy Inauguration, an occasion intended exclusively for fun. President Kennedy was present and made some remarks. At the head table was the chief justice of the Supreme Court. At the tables below the dais were judges, lawyers, diplomats, military people, senators, and members of the House of Representatives. The president remarked that he had heard disapproving comments about his appointment of his brother as attorney general, but, he said, "It seems to me that he should have a little bit of legal experience before he begins his practice of law."

This landed like a ton of concrete on that particular audience and drew only a ripple of laughter out of the crowd.

Robert, however, grew to be an effective and hard-working attorney general.

It was early in our Washington ministry that we discovered serenity and rejuvenation in our vacation home in Nova Scotia. This place, a rich symphony of sights and sounds, not only gave me the necessary opportunity once a year to unwind, but it became through the years an essential part of our family life—one of the few things that actually worked to keep our family together.

The National Presbyterian Church, since the days of Teunis Hamlin, had granted its pastor two months of vacation. During my first weeks in the new pulpit in Washington, I was given the wise advice, "You're given two months vacation. *Use it.*" I soon learned the value of that advice. For with all the responsibilities of my position in Washington, Nova Scotia offered me the opportunity for two months each summer to reacquaint myself with my family.

Even then, I realize I often used the time for other work—mostly working on sermons for the winter program, mailing home topics to the organist, around which he could plan the music for the choir, phoning my staff when decisions needed to be made, and writing articles and books—but it was a different sort of work, and I tried to carve out, nonetheless, time to invest in my family.

In Cape Breton I watched my family grow up—Ellie and Beverly and Mary Faith and David—first reading them stories, such as the local folklore from Neil McNeil's *The Highland Heart in Nova Scotia.* Later, I listened to them discuss their lives and the issues of the day, being amazed at the ways their opinions so often differed from my own, yet impressed with how well their opinions were argued and formed.

The togetherness of these weeks in Cape Breton put deep roots into the characters of our children. (To our immediate family of four children, we have now added three young adult grandchildren—Robin and Eric Heginbotham and Melanie Beth MacRae, who love our other home in the north as their parents and grandparents loved it through the years.)

Our first child, Eleanor, had appeared on the scene in all her regal dignity as the little princess of our La Jolla manse, destined to become the homecoming queen of Wooster College and a diplomatic lady in various American embassies across the world. She became an avid reader, a perennial poet, and a creative writer. Fastidious, precise, and industrious, her goal has always been excellence. Today, with her great love of the English language and English literature, she inspires in her students a high level of scholarship and creativity.

Beverly, twenty-one months younger, grew to be quick in movement, swift in action, and endowed with rhythmic grace. Conscientious and talented, she has always been restless until she reaches the fulfillment of whatever goal she has set for herself. She is a scholar in the field of art, a university professor, an administrator of great ability, a realtor, a dabbler in interior decoration and remodeling, and a lover of great music. Today, she and her lawyer husband, Frank, have put down their roots for lifelong careers in Washington.

Mary Faith was the member of our family who crossed the continent with us by train from California in a doll bed. While especially loved by the whole Washington congregation, the business and professional women of the church made her their choice pet from the time she could toddle into the church hall until this very day. From the beginning Mary Faith was a happy, radiant, sparkling, impish little girl whose friendship was outgoing but whose wrath was fierce and strong when she confronted anything unfair or unjust. Today she is a highly skilled legal secretary and a part-time author.

Into this family of females, in 1950, was born a long-awaited red-haired son who brought much joy into our lives as a child and now, in adulthood, brings balance and stability to the family. He was born at a time that made him one of the sixties generation and gave me an insight into that age and the lives of my parishioners I could never have learned from anyone else. David is a religious person in the profoundest sense. He not only has a grasp of Christian truth but his knowledge extends to an understanding of comparative religions, Christian deviations, and assorted cults. A student of philosophy, history, and the contemporary human scene, David is an intense lover

173

of nature and an avid conservationist. He and his wife, Kathy, have a home on the banks of the Potomac.

Nova Scotia became our home away from home. We learned its history and loved its people. Here we developed lifelong friends, and with those friends, responsibilities. I gave the sermon at the funeral of Donald Nicholson, father of Irene, the young woman who died on the day Eisenhower died.

The church in Little Narrows offered us the chance to be parishioners in another congregation. And Dr. McKinnon, the pastor, offered me the opportunity to sit under another's preaching, and fine preaching at that.

Nova Scotia provided a better value system for our family. Cape Breton is a place where nobody owns much. Its simplicity was a valuable balance to the more formal, sophisticated lives we led in Washington.

And so this land of rivers and lakes and ocean shores and unspoiled fields and forests teeming with wildlife has been our oasis for four decades. In its own way, it became a part of our Christian growth.

As was the case with so many American families, the shadow of America's military adventure in Vietnam hung perilously over our family. There were two periods when as many as five family members were living in Saigon.

Our son-in-law, Erland Heginbotham, a foreign service specialist in Asian affairs, was on the American embassy staff in Saigon. Eleanor taught in the International School. Their daughter Robin was just a small girl at the time, and Eric, our only grandson, was born in the Seventh Day

Adventist Hospital in Saigon. Our Beverly taught English at the Buddhist University and for a time wrote a column in the *Saigon Post*.

Twice they had to be speedily evacuated from the country—on one occasion because of the assassination of President Ngo Dinh Diem.

Ministers and members of American churches were divided by the moral implications of the United States' involvement in Vietnam. Many denominations suffered severe splits. Year in and year out, the National Council of Churches created resolutions and study materials pleading for the U.S. to get out of Vietnam.

In 1967 I was named to a special committee of the Presbyterian General Assembly to study the Vietnam War. After months of work, we drew up a concise, readable summary of the development of American policy in Vietnam—what we felt to be a useful overview of the history of the conflict—titled *Vietnam—the Gospel, the Cross and the Church*.

Our only son, David, during this time had declared himself a conscientious objector and volunteered to work out equivalent service for several years in a community service group in San Diego. I remember his long hours of work, performing menial tasks and hot, difficult jobs, all for mere subsistence pay but no salary. I supported David in his stand of objection to the war, even though my views were different. I believe he helped me see and understand better the concerns and consciences of many others who were also conscientious objectors.

In September of 1967, while Helen and I were enjoying

175

an evening by the fire in our summer home in Nova Scotia, I received a call from the White House. I was asked if I would accept President Johnson's appointment to go to Vietnam as part of an American team to observe the forthcoming elections. As I told Helen the news, she said, "If the president is asking you to go to Vietnam, then you must go to Vietnam."

And so I went. Under the escort of Ambassador Henry Cabot Lodge and oriented by General Westmoreland, our party visited various towns and villages and studied the arrangements being made there for the elections. Later Governor Hughes of New Jersey commented that he wished elections in America could be carried out with the same efficiency.

Returning to Washington, the group was taken to the White House for debriefing by the president. Later I had opportunity to meet with the president alone. I told President Johnson that it was evident to me he was being "done in" by the press and media. Reporters could be seen roaming the country, scavenging for stories of war atrocities or making dangerous generalizations from trivial and isolated reports from Southeast Asia. The president told me that many others had said much the same thing. The media seemed ready to believe anybody except the United States military, the government, or the president.

My views on the Vietnam elections were later featured in the Congressional Record at the request of Senator Gale McGee of Wyoming. Generally speaking, I felt there were three options for the United States at that point in the Vietnam conflict: (1) Escalate the war radically, to the point where it might be won in a day or so. Of course, such an action would render North Vietnam a land of desolation. (2) Withdraw from Vietnam immediately. This would likely yield a holocaust as Vietcong and North Vietnamese would slaughter those who fought against them. (3) Remain in Vietnam with a restraint force and sufficient offensive to win a negotiated just peace. In this case we would "buy time" for the fledgling South Vietnamese government.

I felt that the third option was the only reasonable and moral choice. I believed then, and believe now, that sometimes the failure to use force can be immoral. The possession of power itself holds its responsibilities.

However, America withdrew, and South Vietnam collapsed as a viable state. The world continues to study the meaning of that terrible time. We pray that our children will never be confronted by another Vietnam.

Throughout my ministry I have seemed always to move into a new set of heavy responsibilities before relinquishing the position already held. Thus there were periods, not always brief, when I carried the stress of more than one major activity at a single time.

My only period of complete detachment from work occurred in 1964 when a devastating attack of rheumatoid arthritis forced my hospitalization for surgery and absence from the pulpit for six months of convalescence. Recovery was slow, but late that year Helen and I were able to leave our summer retreat in Nova Scotia and begin the drive back to Washington to resume work in the church.

We were leisurely making our way south through New Hampshire when Helen suddenly saw a sign modestly pointing to GRAY LEDGES. We decided on the spur of the moment to visit this retreat center of which we had heard much. Because it was late in the season, we wondered if it would be open or if anyone would be available. This concern was soon dissipated as we came upon our dear friend, Abraham Vereide, who was resting after a series of summer conferences. He welcomed us warmly, and we had a relaxed conversation. In this casual atmosphere, Abraham suddenly interjected, "You know, Edward, you are to be the next chaplain of the Senate, and I have it on good authority."

Emerging as I was from six months of pain and convalescence, this message came as a fresh anointing of the Holy Spirit and healing grace. Such an expression of confidence in my ministry and Abraham's expectation for my future were just what I needed. At every turn in my life I have felt God's guidance and welcomed whatever the future held. I eagerly resumed my work in the church. The building program for the National Presbyterian Church and Center was moving steadily forward.

On February 8, 1969, while attending an all-day meeting of one of the national agencies of the church, convened in the Mayflower Hotel, I was summoned to the telephone just after lunch. On the line was Senator Gale McGee of Wyoming, who began by congratulating me as the Senate chaplain nominee. He had just come out of the democratic caucus and the Senators had voted to make me their next chaplain to succeed Frederick Brown Harris, who only a few days before had informed the party leaders that he would not accept another term of office.

"In the caucus," Senator McGee informed me, "Senator Stennis made the principal nominating speech and I made the seconding speech." Another candidate, the Reverend Edward Lewis, pastor of the Capitol Hill Methodist Church who had often assisted Dr. Harris, was nominated by Senator Metcalf. The caucus took a secret ballot resulting in my designation as the choice of the majority party. Senator McGee expressed the hope that I would accept the nomination and exercise my ministry in this high legislative body.

My meeting in the Mayflower continued throughout the day and adjourned at five. As I walked through the lobby, I paused to pick up a copy of the Evening Star and was startled to see across five columns of the front page: DR. EDWARD L. R. ELSON TO BE NEW SENATE CHAPLAIN.

When I reached the manse, I displayed the paper to my family. My teenage son, David, was curious to know what my duties might be, and whether we would be leaving the church.

At about eight o'clock that evening the telephone rang, and the Senate secretary, Mr. Francis R. Valeo, asked to speak with me. "Dr. Elson, I suppose you read the papers, and if you read today's Star you know that the Democratic Senate Caucus has chosen you for the office of chaplain of the United States Senate. It is my duty to ask you if you will accept the position."

179

"It will be a great honor," I said to Mr. Valeo, "to be chaplain of the Senate, and you may be sure I will accept the office."

"Very well, then. Report to the Senate tomorrow morning, prepared to take the oath of office, and bring with you a copy of the prayer with which you will open the Senate."

Such was my abrupt induction as Senate chaplain. Fortunately I had been guest chaplain on a number of occasions both in the House and in the Senate and felt quite at home with procedures in the Capitol.

I took the oath of office and ascended the steps of the platform with the president pro tem, Senator Richard Russell of Georgia, who introduced me for my first prayer as chaplain. During the next two years I would be drawn close to the senator in his long terminal bout with cancer.

That day I became the forty-ninth chaplain of the United States Senate. Since then I have made 1,759 convening prayers for the Senate.

I learned later that Vice President Humphrey had taken the time on his way to represent the president at the funeral of Trygve Lie, United Nations secretary general, to telephone Richard Russell: "This is the time to elect Dr. Elson chaplain."

On the day I reported to him, Senator Russell clasped my hand and said, "Dr. Elson, we're certainly happy to welcome you here as our chaplain. It's about time we had a 'homegrown boy' in this office. You know, you're the first American-born chaplain since 1928."

My immediate predecessors were born either in England or Scotland. The chaplaincy had been the one nonpartisan office in the Senate. After a pastorate of twenty-one years in a conspicuous Washington church, I was readily identifiable and did not require an introduction on the Senate floor.

There was one possible problem in the Senate's selection of me as chaplain. My youngest brother Roy had been a democratic candidate for the Senate from Arizona, running earlier against Governor Fannin and later against Senator Goldwater. Senator Carl Curtis was therefore asked to confer with Senator Goldwater to ask how he would feel about having Roy Elson's brother praying over him every day in the Senate. The senator, always a magnanimous gentleman, replied, "The Elsons and Goldwaters have been friends for many years. We have lived together and worked together on a good many things. I can think of nothing finer than having Dr. Elson as chaplain of the Senate, and I would like the privilege of seconding the nomination."

January 9, 1969, was as important a day in my life as it was in the lives of three young men just returned from the moon. It was my first day as chaplain of the Senate. I reported to the Senate lobby and offered the following prayer:

O Lord, . . . as [on] this day we render high honor to the intrepid voyagers in the vast ranges of Thy universe, make us explorers of the spirit and pioneers in a new order of brotherhood and of peace. Equip the people of this land and their representatives here assembled with justice and righteousness, with wisdom and courage, with compassion and mercy, that they may be the servants of Thy purposes upon this earth. Make us good enough, great enough, and strong enough for the age in which we live. . . . Amen.

The prayer concluded, the Senate adopted two or three routine resolutions and then formed a column of twos, headed by the sergeant at arms, the president pro tem, and the secretary. At the end of the line were the remaining officers of the Senate and the Senate staff. The procession crossed the Capitol building to the House Chamber for the purpose of honoring the astronauts who had so recently returned from the moon: Frank Borman, James A. Lovell, Jr., and William N. Anders.

The rules of the Senate prescribe that the daily sessions of that body be convened with prayer by the chaplain. The prayers appear as the first item in the Senate Record. Six books of my Senate prayers have been printed and distributed, and many seem to have had a compounded outreach as they have appeared in church periodicals, on Christmas cards, and several times a year on the front page of the *Wall Street Journal* and as the thought for the day in the *New York Times.*

A special assistant to the president, Dr. Theodore Marrs, had a prayer of mine pasted on his White House phone. Dr. Marrs distributed this prayer widely to his associates:

O Thou who withholds no good gift from those who walk uprightly and call upon Thee with sincere hearts, help us this day to think upon what is true and just and righteous in Thy sight. Grant us grace to speak prudently when we must speak, to remain silent when we have nothing to say, to learn by listening, to be unafraid of the hard decision, to act according to Thy will, and to leave the consequences to Thy Providence. Reward our faithfulness by souls at peace with Thee. . . .

Another who seemed touched by my prayers was Nelson Rockefeller. I became fond of Nelson and his wife, Happy. At public ceremonies where he was to speak and I was to pray, the Rockefellers occasionally took me along in their car. The more I was with Vice President Rockefeller, the better I came to know and understand him, and the more I came to feel he was one of the best qualified men in America for the office of president. He was unafraid of tough problems. If he could not solve them, he engaged the expert who could point the way to a solution. He never turned his back on any assignment because it was too hard. When I finished a prayer in the Senate, he would sometimes say, "Would you let me have that card?" and he would stick it in his pocket.

We were well established in our Washington church when the young Senator Hubert Humphrey arrived from Minnesota with his hardworking young staff. While some few thought him glib and effervescent, those who knew him well and worked closely with him—both friend and political foe—were aware that he was the master of his political philosophy and that his writing and speaking were substantive and profound. He was outgoing and had a radiant disposition. Helen's cousin, Miles Clark, son of the famous author Glenn Clark, came with him as one of his aides for several years. In my early days in

Washington, he and Republican Senator Martin of Pennsylvania frequently inserted my Sunday sermons in the Congressional Record, had them reprinted, and circulated them among their constituencies. I had many long visits with Vice President Humphrey, and when he became ill I visited with him. At his death, I conducted a private service for family and staff and led the prayers at his national memorial service in the Rotunda of the Capitol.

When I became chaplain of the Senate, a bipartisan committee consisting of Democratic senators Mansfield and Stennis and Republican senators Dirksen and Bennett was formed to redefine the office and role of the Senate chaplain.

The first communication I had from the committee was to say that we would have no guest chaplains in the Senate until further authority was given by this committee. I was to give all the prayers and perform all the duties of chaplain until otherwise informed. I worked with the committee, and we developed a policy that provided that the convening prayer would be limited to two minutes. It would be given exclusively in the English language. It would be free from sectarianism, partisan politics, and intimations about foreign policy.

At the end of five months, the committee resumed the practice of inviting guest chaplains, though not to exceed two in any month. The reason for this limitation was that many invited clergymen, representing ethnic groups or contentious political lobbies, had been addressing their prayers to Almighty God but hoping the senators would hear and heed them. To have guest chaplains was a good practice when properly managed. Senators enjoyed the privilege of nominating clergymen from their home states to serve as guest chaplains.

A few senators were annoyed by the new rule. In the church, as well as in the army, I had learned something of the manifold ways by which some climb the ecclesiastical ladder. It was not hard to develop a list of prospective guest chaplains with one hundred senators and hosts of others making recommendations, and I endeavored to be fair to representatives of many denominations in our pluralistic culture. It meant a great deal to each guest chaplain and to his family to be honored by an invitation and to receive a handsome certificate, signed by the vice president, the secretary, and the chaplain of the Senate. It was my practice to invite our guest chaplain to dine with his senator in the Senate dining room.

During my twelve years and one month as chaplain, a long history of exclusively male participation was broken when the Reverend Dr. Wilmina Rowland of Philadelphia, a Presbyterian clergywoman, led us in the opening prayer in July 1974. Later that month, a Roman Catholic nun, Sister Joan Keleher Doyle of the Sisters of Charity of the Blessed Virgin Mary, offered the prayer.

It was an exciting day at the United States Capitol when, for the first time in history, an American Indian Chief, Holy Man Chief Crow of the Sioux Indians in

South Dakota, was the honored guest of the Senate. The chief was ninety years of age and was nominated by Senator Abourezk.

The South Dakota Sioux people had come upon troublesome times and violence threatened hour by hour. When we were making the arrangements for the chief's appearance, we learned that he would pray only in the Sioux language. To do that would infringe upon two Senate rules—the one requiring English as the sole language of the prayer, and the other limiting the delivery to two minutes, because the interpreter would double the time. When I made this known to the two party leaders of the Senate, both of them—Mansfield and Scott—said that if there was ever a time in American history to set aside the rules for the opening prayer, this was the occasion.

Chief Crow was an impressive figure in his leather jacket, matching slacks, moccasins, and full headpiece of magnificent feathers. He did not come alone, for more than two hundred Sioux braves converged on Washington and occupied a place in the Senate gallery directly across the chamber from the presiding officer's desk where the chief would stand to pray. Somehow one of the Senate doorkeepers discovered that the Sioux had one or more Sioux flags that they expected to break out in the afterglow of the chief's prayer. After a tussle, during which the flags were confiscated, the time for the prayer had arrived.

The chief's prayer was translated by another Indian, Matthew King, who spoke flawless English. As Chief Crow spoke, he lifted his peace pipe from earth to heaven, paused, then lifted the pipe from north to south, paused again, then moved it from east to west.

The chief was reverent, and there was about him an air of wonder as he stretched out his arms and lifted his face heavenward. Members of the Senate stood in hushed reverence throughout the prayer and its translation. Chief Crow prayed that the Great Spirit would impart wisdom and strength to these "young men" for their heavy burdens as they soared on this orb called earth throughout the immeasurable regions of unending space. Somehow or other, when the prayer was over, everyone present felt supported and uplifted by the Great Spirit.

Several senators then took the floor to express appreciation for the Indians and their chief. Soon I escorted the holy man to the steps of the Capitol building, where we were joined by Senator Abourezk and surrounded by several hundred Indians who were no longer the quiet and docile young men who had just been in the Senate Chamber. After the photographs and press interviews, they broke up in small groups and visited their congressmen, just as any other constituents do when they visit the capital.

In March 1973 the Reverend Louis H. Evans, Jr., became the pastor of the National Presbyterian Church. He, too, had been pastor of the church in La Jolla, though not my immediate successor. Louis Evans, Jr., and his wife, Colleen Townsend, form an effective evangelistic team working inside and outside the Presbyterian Church. Their gracious arrangment of the fiftieth anniversary of my ministry made it for us an unforgettable event, and had further significance for many in the congregation that day as we remembered Louis Evans' father, the great preacher from Hollywood, who had been my guest summer preacher in the summers of the Eisenhower presidency.

The Watergate episode took place during my term as chaplain of the Senate, and day by day for several years the work of the entire Congress was slowed and distorted. The Senate committee under the chairmanship of the inimitable Sam Ervin, Jr., the leading constitutional lawyer of the Senate, and with Senator Howard Baker as assistant chairman, held their meetings in the Senate Caucus Room on the third floor of the Russell Office Building. There were several ways to approach this room, but most participants passed the Senate chaplain's office en route. I attended thirty-five or forty of the daily sessions, and many of those who came to testify, including some of the leading figures, came to the chaplain's office to see me on their way to the Caucus Room.

I asked the Lord for wisdom and spiritual insight that I might be a faithful and effective pastor to each of them. Some became my good friends. When court cases were over and men were serving prison terms, several of them kept up a correspondence with me.

We felt very sorry for the Nixons. They were our neighbors in Wesley Heights for about twenty years and their daughters went to school with our David and Mary Faith from kindergarten through junior high school. We stopped by each other's front doors and sometimes even showed up at the same PTA meetings. (Not until we served in Washington did we learn that the Elsons and the Nixons had each been married in the St. Francis Chapel in the Riverside Inn in Riverside, California—Helen and I in February 1937 and the Nixons about five years later.) We had friendly conversations, but I often wished that Richard Nixon had a pastor—a spiritual confidant to whom he could speak and from whom he could hear anything said in love. He had close friends among the clergy, including Billy Graham, but none of them, so far as I could discover, was really a pastor to him in the truest and profoundest sense.

As the hearings went on and the information accumulated, I felt that the significance of Watergate rested not in what it revealed about the culprits, but rather in what it said about America. Americans simply will not tolerate, for long, deviation from the moral law in the commonly accepted terms of the Ten Commandments. The people will have the wayward turn from their evil ways. Justice Oliver Wendell Holmes once said, "The Ten Commandments will not budge," and in the Watergate affair this fact was demonstrated day after day. If you lie, cheat, lust, bear false witness, or think with anger in your heart, you destroy your human personality just as surely as bullets and poison destroy the body.

Both houses of Congress were uneasy about an impeachment process. Such would virtually shut down routine congressional business for many months.

Then, on August 8, 1974, a date I shall never forget, Senators Scott and Goldwater and Congressman Rhodes went to see the president to lay before him the predicament in which he found himself and in which he placed the Congress. While these three emissaries were at the White House, all who knew about their mission surely prayed that somehow the right action would deliver the country from its agonizing ordeal.

That night the president announced to the country that he would resign from the presidency, effective at noon the next day. On August 9, when Gerald Ford was sworn in as the thirty-eighth president of the United States, I offered the following prayer at the opening of the Senate:

God of our fathers and our God, by whose providence this nation was born and by whom we have been guarded and guided, in this hour of mingled tragedy and hope, lift our lives into the clear light of Thy presence and encompass us with Thy love. By the miracle of Thy grace transform this time of sorrow and judgment into a season of cleansing and healing.

Deal graciously, O Lord, with our departing president. Accord him appreciation for every noble achievement, forgiveness for every acknowledged wrong and grant him a new life of usefulness and inner peace. Surround his family with Thy comfort and love.

Grant to Thy servant, Gerald Ford, on this day of dedication, a vivid awareness of Thy presence and the assurance of Thy supporting strength. Endow him plenteously with the sinews of Thy Spirit, with moral courage, with wisdom beyond his own, and with power to lead the republic in reconciliation and unity, in peace and prosperity, in justice and righteousness.

Chastened and cleansed, but full of hope and faith, help us, O God, in our private lives and as a people to walk in the ways of Thy commandments, to live by the truth, to do justly, to love

190

mercy, and to serve Thee with our whole heart and mind and strength that Thy will be done on earth. Amen.

As chaplain of the Senate, I served directly under the vice president of the United States. According to the Constitution, the vice president is the Senate's presiding officer. (In the day-to-day business of the Senate, the president pro tem or his appointee usually presides.)

Spiro T. Agnew was the vice president when I became chaplain. He and his wife were a popular couple on the Washington scene. He was a gifted phrasemaker, which served him well in the ups and downs of his career.

Gerald Ford was a steady craftsman in government. Twenty-five years in the House of Representatives prepared him for dealing with the Congress. Long before the National Prayer Breakfast movement appeared, Gerald Ford and several other Congressmen were holding periodic prayer meetings. I was very fond of him and I shall always feel disappointed that he was not elected president. He proved himself an effective one.

Walter Mondale had the longest term as vice president during my chaplaincy. Both he and his wife were preacher's kids and there was a strong empathy between us. Mondale had a brilliant legal mind, a sensitive conscience to social needs, and was an astute politician. I believe he would have made an able president.

George Bush was vice president when I retired. In the Eisenhower years I came to know his father, who was a capable Senator. George Bush has probably had the most diverse career of any vice president in recent years. Because the chaplain and the vice president appeared frequently on the same programs, there was time for us to become well acquainted.

During this twelve-year period the Senate and its chaplain and other officers had been the object of two legal suits by the professional atheist, Madalyn O'Hair. The first suit in 1973 alleged violation of the First Amendment for praying and quoting the Bible in the Senate and other government buildings. The second suit, filed in 1980, alleged that the First Amendment was transgressed by the Senate electing and maintaining chaplains and providing for the support of that office with government funds.

In a lull in the business of the Senate, when there was a brief recess, I was engaged in conversation with Senator Ervin of North Carolina, to whom I said, "Senator, I may need your help in the courts, for I am being sued by the atheist, O'Hair."

"What would she be suing you about?" he inquired.

"I pray in this chamber and sometimes quote from the Bible."

The senator smiled. "Why doesn't Mrs. O'Hair sue one of us? We have more time to quote the Bible on the floor than you have."

The case was heard by the senior judge of the United States District Federal Court, Judge George L. Hart, Jr., and was promptly dismissed. When I asked him the basis for dismissing the case, he said, "The suit is frivolous, and I do not hear frivolous cases in my court. Moreover Mrs. O'Hair had no legal basis for the suit. Under the constitutional doctrine of the separation of powers, the Senate has exclusive authority over what takes place in its own chambers, who its officers will be, what their duties are, and their compensation."

This is why Senator Ervin earlier had said, "Dr. Elson, you have no need to worry over Mrs. O'Hair's suit. She is not a senator of the United States." The whole subject of chaplains and prayers belongs in the legislative bodies, the House and the Senate, and has no place in the court. However, I am sure this will not be the last we see of such legal actions.

One of the difficult lessons of government service is that one must live in the world as it is. In the case of a senator, this means wrestling with issues that do not always represent a clear choice and working within a system that requires compromise. No vote is 100 percent pure. An issue with which a senator agrees may be tied legislatively to an issue about which he has grave reservations. Which way should he vote?

Senators, consequently, often cannot vote exactly the way they would like. Back home, their voting record may be seriously misunderstood.

This realization has brought us very close to some government leaders caught in these difficult decisions. Some have come to me for counsel and, throughout my ministry as chaplain of the Senate, have become dear friends.

My years of ministry to the Senate as a body, to the individual senators and their families, and to supporting staff members gave me a tender sympathy for and deep insight into the eroding stresses of political life. The people in public office, and all associated with them, become public property to their constituents. Senators have their own pastors "back home," but the Senate chaplain is their on-the-job, ever-available minister in Washington.

One such senator to whom I have felt especially close as a pastor in Washington is Senator John Stennis of Mississippi, known to everyone in the Senate as "Mr. Ethics" and uniformly respected for his character and integrity. Whenever there is a difficult assignment which has to do with the personal conduct of a senator, Senator Stennis is made the chairman of the committee, and he handles the problem fearlessly but with justice and compassion.

In his time of distress, Richard Nixon offered to be guided by the wisdom of "Judge Stennis" if it would relieve the Congress of pursuing impeachment. When Senator Stennis was shot twice and his life hung in the balance, people all over the United States, of all parties and all races, prayed earnestly for his recovery.

I was at his bedside in Walter Reed Hospital and remained there all night with Mrs. Stennis while she awaited the arrival of their daughter and son. Quite a company of senators and reporters gathered in the waiting room, answering questions, taking phone calls, and phoning relatives throughout the night.

Other members of the Senate stand out for their service, morality, and spirituality. I remember a talk by Richard Lugar of Indiana which concerned the role of the Sadducees and the Pharisees in the time of Christ, and their predicament when dealing with matters of law and ethics. Senator Sam Nunn of Georgia, a learned and astute expert in national defense, is a lay leader in the Methodist Church. He was encouraged to take part in the Senate Prayer Group by the senators who preceded him. Senator Herman Talmadge of Georgia was one of the steady personalities at the prayer breakfasts. He asked penetrating questions as a member of the Watergate Committee.

Former senator Harrison Schmidt of New Mexico and Senator John Glenn of Ohio are two former astronauts for whom I shall always be grateful. Schmitt brought to public life the mind of a scientist—a geologist, a chemist, a physicist—and of a dedicated Christian. His was a rare combination of gifts and insights. I once heard him give a teleological argument for the existence of God. I watched him with a group of Boy Scouts. He entertained them with the story of going to the moon and back and with speculations about what is likely to take place in future world history—spaceships, migrations, and vacations to someplace we never dreamed possible.

Senator John Glenn circled the earth in a primitive contraption. When one sees his ship in the Smithsonian Air and Space Museum and contrasts it with the more developed ones today, one realizes the danger of his being incinerated and what a daring thing it was for him to complete that voyage.

Senator James B. Allen of Alabama, at the time of his death in 1978, was chairman of the Senate Prayer Breakfast program. He was a brilliant parliamentarian and an avid student of the English Bible. His funeral was a victorious witness to the Resurrection of Christ. Maryon, his wife, succeeded him in the Senate, but lost the seat in a later election. She remains one of our choicest friends in Washington.

As Great Britain has its Margaret Thatcher, the United States has its women luminaries. Senator Margaret Chase Smith of Maine mastered the art of independent analysis and personal choice. During her lifetime of service in the Senate, she received more than fifty honorary degrees. Nancy Kassenbaum also deserves mention. She now carries on brilliantly in the Senate as she had done in earlier years in Kansas and Washington.

Senators John Stennis and Howard Baker and their families have been close to me and supportive in the life of the National Presbyterian Church. No words can adequately convey my personal estimate of these two men. They have been true leaders in the Senate in all issues where loyalty to their country must transcend political interests. Reared in different generations, their southern values are the same.

While pastoral duties and ceremonial tasks were my primary ministries in the Senate, there were also the day-by-day contacts in offices, cloakrooms, elevators, and passageways when the chaplain is sought for pastoral counseling. There is sickness at home. Someone is seriously ill in the hospital. A senator is shot. A senator's son is accidently electrocuted. A senator dies suddenly. A police officer dies. A page is killed in an airplane wreck. There are state funerals. There are weddings. The chaplain's service reaches not only to one hundred senators and their families, but potentially to thousands who need an on-the-job ministry.

At a time when Christians seemed to identify themselves by their theological differences, it was my job as chaplain to transcend doctrinal diversities that people represented—to be inclusive rather than exclusive—and to minister the grace of God to each and every one who participated in the governmental arena.

One Wednesday morning I arrived at the Vandenberg Room a little early for the Senate Prayer Breakfast. Looking through the door, I saw three men sitting together talking quietly. Between John Stennis and Mark Hatfield sat President Jimmy Carter. All the senators were duly surprised and pleased as they arrived on the scene. As far as I know, this is the only time a president has attended a Senate Prayer Breakfast at the Capitol.

One of the difficult responsibilities of any pastor is the business of conducting funerals. For a Senate chaplain, this task is under public scrutiny. Sometimes it can be rather eventful. After Senator Russell died, we were flying to his Georgia home when the whole area was seized with a violent storm, making it impossible for the fleet of planes bearing the Senate party to reach its destination. There was constant radio communication as preparations for the funeral continued and the service was undertaken in the local church and cemetery. Senator Mansfield was to have a part in the service, Senator Stennis was to deliver the eulogy, and I was to read the

Scripture and offer a prayer. When it was certain we would not be able to reach the church and cemetery, our plane was brought down in Charleston, South Carolina, and the two senators and I were rushed through the city streets with sirens blaring to a television studio from which our part of the funeral was transmitted to the crowds at the church and cemetery.

Another quite memorable funeral was that of Senator Dirksen. I shall never forget the throngs of people, especially the children, lining the route of the motorcade from the airport to the church in Pekin, Illinois, Senator Dirksen's hometown. Dirksen was the silver-tongued orator, almost the last of the species, who with just one speech could change a Senate vote. All his life, he developed the skills of an orator and built an effective vocabulary. As a young officer in World War I, having only stale magazines and a Bible to read, he memorized great passages from the Bible and used them flawlessly in his public utterances. Late in life he made recordings of the Bible for the public market.

He died on the Sunday the National Presbyterian Church held its first service in the new church building. When I reached Walter Reed Hospital to comfort Mrs. Dirksen and her daughter Joy, the first thing Mrs. Dirksen said was, "Can we have his funeral service in the new church?" We assured her that would be possible.

Thus on the following Wednesday morning we had the entire leadership of the United States government assembled in the church to honor the great statesman from Illinois.

Fortunately, the government parish also has its share of romances and weddings to celebrate.

Cliff Robertson was in our youth program in the La Jolla church where I baptised him when he was a small boy. It was not surprising then that when the actor Cliff was to marry the actress Dina Merrill in Hillwood, the Washington home of Dina's mother, they asked me to officiate at their wedding. It was a special joy to me that Cliff and Dina returned to Washington on the occasion of the fiftieth anniversary of my ordination. Cliff read the Scriptures and spoke of my ministry to him in his boy-hood. Another happy experience of that Sunday was to see in my congregation Jeanette and Harry Bimber, the first couple married by me, with their forty-five-year-old son. They had come from California to Washington to mark the fiftieth anniversary of their marriage and the fiftieth anniversary of my ordination.

Through the years I have kept up a correspondence with couples I have married. For those whom we see frequently, such as the popular Washington columnist Betty Beale and George Graeber, there is a special warmth and affection.

Only members of Congress and officials of the Capitol are eligible for marriage in the Capitol Prayer Room. Thus the architect of the Capitol, George White, and his bride, Suzanne Neiley, were married in the Capitol Prayer Room by the two congressional chaplains, Edward Elson and Edward Latch.

Romance blossomed on Capitol Hill when Senator Robert Dole and Transportation Secretary Elizabeth Dole were united in marriage by me in a chapel of Washington Cathedral. In World War II Bob Dole had been a teenage soldier in the Seventy-fifth Infantry Division when I was the division chaplain. He became an infantry officer, was severely wounded, and after recovery began his great political career.

For twelve years and one month, I served as Senate chaplain. They were joyous years.

In 1981 I retired from the Senate chaplaincy. The Reverend Richard Halverson succeeded me. Dr. Halverson is a well-known minister among evangelicals and is active in the Prayer Breakfast movement. I had nominated him for the pastorate of the Fourth Presbyterian Church, which for more than twenty years he served with distinction. He has been a friend of mine for many years.

As the army never separated me from the church, nor the church from my army ministry, so my parishes in church and Senate were an overlapping ministry. I carried with me the same gospel, and the needs of those to whom I have ministered have been the same needs. God has led me in pleasant pastures as he has allowed me to feed his sheep.

Epilogue

What do I say in the glimmering twilight of a long ministry, forty years of which were based in Washington? How do I convey my thanksgiving for being allowed the role of undershepherd of the great Shepherd in the pastures of the Spirit?

Since that day when, by the laying on of the hands of Presbytery, I was ordained to be a minister of word and sacrament, I have endeavored to be faithful to that ministry. I have preached the gospel in country churches, on street corners with the Salvation Army, in the great cathedrals of many continents, such as St. John's Cathedral in New York and St. Giles Cathedral in Edinburgh, I have celebrated the Sacrament on the hood of a jeep and the landing ramp of an LST. I have lectured at theological conferences, seminaries, and institutes. But it has everywhere been the same gospel. Circumstances of time and place have given me a unique ministry to some leaders of our national government. At all times there were in my congregation presidents, high-ranking government and military officials, visitors from other countries, leaders in industry and education, and scores of people working with hand and brain in the routine duties of daily life.

Need I say that I believe in the institutional church? God has used the church through the centuries as the means for transmitting the gospel to the world. His ministers are sustained by the body of Christ, the whole family of believers.

In the church we learn the truths about God and man and human destiny. The layman in the political arena, no less than the pastor and evangelist, must live out his days as a "born of the Spirit" authentic Christian in the life of the church.

God is a God of history. He works in and through history. When man, because of his perversity, by himself could not lift himself, God took the initiative. And in this is our hope. God sent His Son who revealed all we can know of God in human terms. He lived as no other person ever lived. He died on a cross for our redemption.

"There was no other good enough to pay the price of sin. He only could unlock the gate of heaven and let us in. Oh dearly, dearly has He loved, and we must love Him too and trust in His redeeming grace and try His work to do."

When I retired from the pastorate of the National Presbyterian Church in 1973, a monument wall in front of the church was unveiled and dedicated to my ministry, bearing an inscription cut in stone:

Let your bearing towards one another arise out of your life in Christ Jesus. For the divine nature was his from the first; yet he

did not think to snatch at equality with God, but made himself nothing, assuming the nature of a slave. Bearing the human likeness, revealed in human shape, he humbled himself, and in obedience accepted death—death on a cross. Therefore God raised him to the heights and bestowed on him the name above all names, that at the name of Jesus every knee should bow—in heaven, on earth, and in the depths—and every tongue confess, "Jesus Christ is Lord," to the glory of God the Father. Philippians 2:5-11
The New English Bible

This has been the cornerstone of my life and ministry.

My ministry has transcended a single denomination, and my message has been to a broad spectrum of believers.

At a meeting of the General Assembly of the United Presbyterian Church of North America, I was the guest preacher. The assembly business sessions were over and we were in the climactic service of a historic convocation. I was moved to preach on the resurrection of Jesus Christ, the central theme of our faith: "Christ is risen. Christ is risen. Hallelujah!" As I finished, I felt that God was using me in the power of the Holy Spirit.

When the sermon was ended, the choir rendered the magnificent "Hallelujah Chorus" from Handel's *Messiah.* The choirmaster led the singers and instrumentalists with spirited gestures, and the result was a rendition of triumphal beauty and power. It was a high event, for some a preview of the great chorus at the end of time when the redeemed will be singing hallelujahs to the sovereign God and Father and to His Son, Jesus Christ our Lord.

In this exalted moment the choirmaster collapsed. The

music continued: ". . . and He shall reign forever and ever." The director's body was conveyed to the choir room. A doctor came. Soon the pastor emerged to say the director had just made the crossing and even now was rejoicing with the redeemed on the other side. He was with his Lord.

That chorus never ceases. That message is never silenced. The visible and the invisible, the temporal and the eternal know no distinction.

So let us lift high the cross, unfurl the flags, herald the gospel. "He shall reign forever and ever and ever. Hallelujah." Amen.

Acknowledgments

My deep gratitude goes to Catharine Hauberg Sweeney, long-time friend and neighbor in Washington, in Coconut Grove, and in Cape Breton, who provided the cottage in her Florida kampong where most of this book took shape.

My sincere thanks to Wendell Hawley for his sustained enthusiasm for this personal history, and to Ken Petersen for skillful editing and wise counseling, and to Ray Varisco who expedited the early movement of this manuscript.

Special appreciation goes to my daughter, Mary Faith Elson MacRae, who with unbounded love and with marked skill, through many drafts, prepared the manuscript for publication.

Thanks to Eleanor Elson Heginbotham and Beverly Elson Gray for loving professional attention to this unfolding story.

Thanks to two brothers, Roy and Howard Elson, for accompanying me on a pilgrimage, retracing our boy-

hood paths in western Pennsylvania with video camera
and tape recorder.

Thanks to Donald Holmes who helped refine the narrative of my World War II experiences, and to three women
for an all-night session to meet a publisher's deadline:
Mordena Millar, Wilmyrna Smith, and Doreen Durant.

My abiding gratitude goes to Thomas A. Stone, friend
of many years and three times my colleague in the pastorate, unexcelled specialist in religious education and
founder of the famed Sunday Evening Club of Washington.

"Blest be the tie that binds" my heart in abiding friendship with Edward A. Latch and James Ford, my associates
in the congressional chaplaincy.

My public ministry to historic figures is given more
attention than my relationship to the hundreds of families who gave daily meaning and joy to my life and that
of our family: to my elder Howard Edson, superior
church parliamentarian and support in my early days in
Washington; to Dr. Irvin Chapman, the greatest Clerk of
Session I ever knew, and his wife, Dr. Elizabeth Kahler,
not only superior leaders in the life of the church but for
us the loving professional friends who guarded the lives
of each member of our family; and to our family doctor,
Dr. Walter K. Myers and his wife, Carol Grosvenor
Myers, and her parents, Dr. and Mrs. Gilbert Grosvenor,
who opened to us their homes in Washington and Florida
and introduced us to summers in Nova Scotia in a relationship as close as that of family; and to Edward and
Catharine Sweeney with whom we have traveled great

distances and lived intimately, sharing the pivotal experiences of family life: the raising of our children, marriages, illness, and death.

Thanks to our Cape Breton pastors, the Reverend Alexander MacDonald and the Reverend Donald Sutherland, who have nourished our spirits and given us pastoral care beyond the call of duty.

My deep appreciation goes to two special friends—Freeman H. Carey, M.D., Attending Physician, United States Capitol, and Watson Sodero, M.D., of Cape Breton—both of whom treated the mind and spirit, as well as the body.

A salute to three young men whose clergymen fathers honored me by giving their sons my name in Christian baptism: Edward Elson Farquhar of Montreal, Edward Elson Laidlaw of North Carolina, and David Edward Elson Poling of West Virginia.

A grand salute to Edouard Neis-berger, one of the foremost organists of the world, who played brilliantly at my fiftieth anniversary.

Sincere thanks to my personal secretaries whose technical skills and personal wisdom were of immeasurable assistance in my ministry: serving me while pastor of the National Presbyterian Church—Sarah Davidson, Ellen McCaw, Thelma Livingston, Mary MacRae, and Marjorie Cook; assisting me in the Senate chaplaincy—Kitty Diaz, Thelma Abbott, and Allie Johnson.

Most of all, my abiding thanks to Helen who with patience and tenderness encouraged this work and without whom it would never have been completed.

My pastorate of twenty-seven years in the National Presbyterian Church was enhanced by the service of colleagues who served as Associate Ministers at various periods: James F. Lundquist, John B. Hayes, Thomas A. Stone, John J. Rice, Harold E. Meyers, John Vedder Edwards, Roderic Lee Smith, Richard E. Robinson, Thomas P. Luce, and two Princeton Theological Seminary students—Lacy Harwell and Frank Watson—who performed valuable services and gave the congregation faith in the future leadership of the church.